The E•Z Legal Guide to

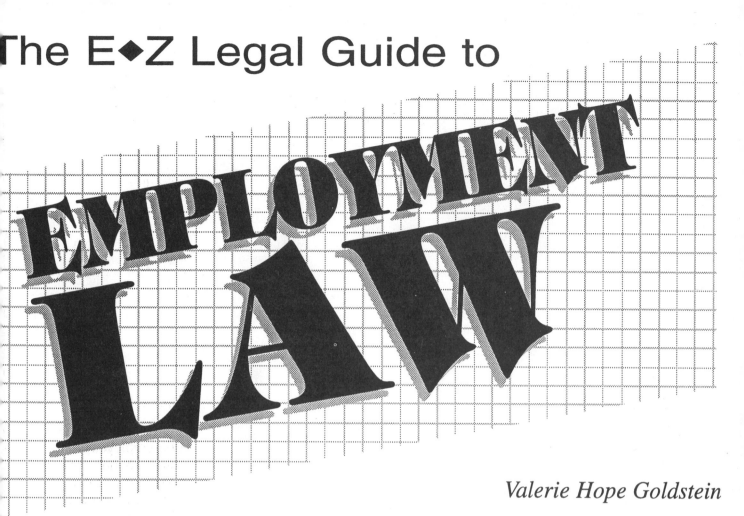

EMPLOYMENT LAW

Valerie Hope Goldstein

D0565808

E•Z Legal Books

Deerfield Beach, Florida

Copyright 1995, E-Z Legal Forms, Inc.
Printed in the United States of America

E·Z LEGAL FORMS®

384 South Military Trail Deerfield Beach, FL 33442
Tel. 954-480-8933 Fax 954-480-8906
All rights reserved.
Distributed by E-Z Legal Forms, Inc.
...when you need it in writing! is a registered trademark of E-Z Legal Forms, Inc.

... when you need it in writing!®

4 5 6 7 8 9 10   CPC

Library of Congress Catalog Card Number: 94-061868

The E-Z Legal Guide to Employment Law
Written by Valerie Hope Goldstein

        p.   cm.

ISBN 1-56382-412-4: $14.95

 I. Goldstein, Valerie Hope, author.
 II. Title: The E-Z Legal Guide to Employment Law.

Important facts

E-Z Legal products are designed to provide authoritative and accurate information in regard to the subject matter covered. However, neither this nor any other publication can take the place of an attorney on important legal matters.

Information in this guide has been carefully compiled from sources believed to be reliable, but the accuracy of the information is not guaranteed, as laws and regulations may change or be subject to differing interpretations.

Why not have your attorney review this guide? We encourage it.

Limited warranty and disclaimer

This is a self-help legal product and is intended to be used by the consumer for his or her own benefit. Use of this product to benefit a second party may be considered the unauthorized practice of law.

As with any legal matter, common sense should determine whether you need the assistance of an attorney. We urge you to consult with an attorney whenever large amounts of money are involved or on any matter when you do not understand how to properly complete a form or question its adequacy to protect you.

It is understood that by using this legal guide you are acting as your own attorney. Accordingly, the publisher, author, distributor and retailer shall have neither liability nor responsibility to any party for any loss or damage caused or alleged to be caused by use of this guide. This guide is sold with the understanding that the publisher, author, distributor and retailer are not engaged in rendering legal services. If legal services or other expert assistance are required, the services of a competent professional should be sought.

Money-back guarantee

E-Z Legal Forms offers you a limited guarantee. If E-Z Legal Forms are found to be defective, you may return your purchase to us within 30 days for a full refund of the list or purchase price, whichever is lower. In no event shall our liability – or the liability of any retailer – exceed the purchase price of the product. Use of the product constitutes acceptance of these terms.

Copyright Permission Certificate

Employment Law

Table
of contents

How to use this E-Z Legal Guide

E-Z Legal Guides can help you achieve an important legal objective conveniently, efficiently and economically. But it is nevertheless important for you to properly use this guide if you are to avoid later difficulties.

Step-by-step instructions for using this guide:

1 Carefully read all information, warnings and disclaimers concerning the legal forms in this guide. If after thorough examination you decide that you have circumstances that are not covered by the forms in this guide, or you do not feel confident about preparing your own documents, consult an attorney.

2 Before filling out a form, make several copies of the original to practice on, to submit to the courts and for future use and updates. **All documents submitted to the court must be printed on one side only.** You should also make copies of the completed forms. Create a record-keeping system for both sets of copies.

3 Complete each blank on each legal form. Do not skip over inapplicable blanks or lines intended to be completed. If the blank is inapplicable, mark "N/A" or "None" or use a dash. This shows you have not overlooked the item.

4 Always use pen or type on legal documents. Never use pencil.

5 Avoid erasing or crossing out anything you've written on final documents.

6 It is important to remember that on legal contracts or agreements between parties all terms and conditions must be clearly stated. Provisions may not be enforceable unless in writing. All parties to the agreement should receive a copy.

7 You may find more specific instructions within this guide for completing some forms. These instructions are for your benefit and protection, so follow them closely.

8 You will find a helpful glossary of terms at the end of this guide. Refer to this glossary if you encounter unfamiliar terms.

9 Always keep legal documents in a safe place and in a location known to your spouse, family, personal representative or attorney.

Introduction to Employment Law

Few legal fields have witnessed as many changes as has employment law. New laws and policies such as Affirmative Action, the Americans with Disabilities Act, COBRA, ERISA, and the Equal Pay Act have been responsible for changing the relationship between employers and employees. All workers have the right to know which laws protect them in the workplace, and employers must be updated on how changes in those laws could affect their companies.

This guide is a broad overview of employment regulations for both employers and employees. There are chapters on hiring and firing, Social Security, taxes, minimum wage, overtime, benefits, discrimination, unions, OSHA and most of the other subjects of concern in the workplace today.

Another purpose of this guide is to foster communication. Misunderstandings and lawsuits can be avoided if employers and employees take the time to discuss each other's concerns. Throughout this book you will find pointers for employers and their employees on how to better communicate with each other.

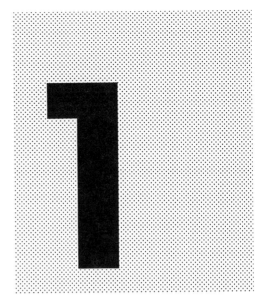

Recruiting and hiring

Discrimination in hiring has become a major issue in the last two decades. Although hiring abuses are illegal, employers continue to screen out qualified job applicants based on such illegal criteria as age, race, and gender.

Illegal classified ads

Discrimination is often evident at the earliest stage of recruitment. Consider these Help Wanted ads from a local paper:

"Able-bodied, recent college grad wanted for secretarial work..."

"Girl Friday needed..."

"Young, ambitious, single professional sought by agency..."

These ads are probably similar to hundreds of classifieds that are printed every day. They are illegal because they discourage certain groups from applying for the jobs. An employer must avoid biased language in recruitment advertising, including any terms that discriminate by age, gender, race, religion, national origin, marital status, physical disability, or sexual orientation.

The first ad is an example of disability bias. Its use of the terms "able-bodied" and "recent college grad" implies that the employer is looking for a young, physically fit worker. This discourages older and disabled applicants from applying for the job.

In some cases it is acceptable to specify that the worker be in good shape – for a position requiring heavy lifting, for example. However, this ad is for a secretary, a sedentary job that may be done by employees of any age in almost any physical condition. Therefore, the employer's request for someone young and able-bodied is illegal.

The second ad is an example of gender bias. "Girl Friday" indicates that the employer will not consider male applicants for the position. Not only are males discriminated against in this ad, but it raises the question of whether this employer's gender bias extends to other areas. Would a woman be considered for a management position? Even the usage of the word "girl" as a reference to women may be considered derogatory.

The employer should specify the type of work to be done and use appropriate job titles, such as "Clerical Worker" or "Courier." Under no circumstances should a classified ad show gender preference. While an exception might be made for the recruitment of a live-in director of a single-sex dormitory, words that show preferences or impose limitations must be left out of the advertisement.

The third example indicates age bias because it uses the word "young." The employer demonstrates another bias by using the adjective "single." Such terms are often used to screen out female candidates, particularly those with children or those who plan to have children. Even if there is no gender bias, the ad is still illegal in that the employer is rejecting the resumes of qualified married persons in favor of those who are unmarried.

If a specific salary is mentioned in an ad, the employer must be prepared to pay at least that amount. In recent years courts have held that written company materials, including classified ads promising a specific salary, are a type of contract, and that failing to provide the salary offered in the ad may be a breach of that contract. An employer should have the company personnel officer or attorney review ads before they are placed in the newspaper.

The law requires government contractors to put the words "Equal Opportunity Employer" in job ads. If a labor strike is in progress at the firm, this too must be mentioned in the ad.

What is legal? ▬▬▬▬▬▬▬▬▬▬▬▬▬▬▬▬▬▬▬▬▬▬▬

What may an ad include? Many employers have a written description for each job title. By analyzing the most important duties and requirements of the job to be filled, an employer might specify the following requirements in a classified ad:

1. The education and experience needed for the job

Highlight

An employer should have the company personnel officer or attorney review ads before they are placed in the newspaper.

2) The specific skills required, e.g. typing speed, flower arranging, third-party billing, etc.

3) Experience with specific equipment, e.g. computer software, tools, machinery etc.

4) The salary and benefits being offered

5) The person to contact at the company

6) The required references

<table>
<tr><td>

Highlight

An employment interviewer must balance the need to fully assess an applicant's qualifications with the limitations on what can be asked without risking a lawsuit.

</td><td>

Other options

Employers seeking applicants for a job do not have to place an outside classified ad. While they must usually notify employees within their firm of the job opening by displaying a job notice in a prominent area, they may advertise outside the firm using any method they choose, including word of mouth. However, word-of-mouth advertising sometimes discriminates against certain groups. If most of the firm's employees live in a white section of town and the firm does business there exclusively, word of mouth may not reach qualified black applicants. The Equal Employment Opportunity Commission finds such advertising methods unacceptable.

Some companies choose to have an outside employment agency do their recruiting for them. If a company uses this strategy, it must be sure that the agency understands that the company is an Equal Opportunity Employer and that the agency may not in any way discriminate in its selection of applicants. The agency must also be licensed in the client's state.

</td></tr>
</table>

The interview and the application process

Conducting an employment interview can be a legal minefield. An employment interviewer must balance the need to fully assess an applicant's qualifications with the limitations on what can be asked without risking a lawsuit.

As with the classified ad, the employer wants to avoid looking for qualifications that have nothing to do with the job. Some employers try to find out an applicant's marital and family status, to avoid paying higher health benefits or child care costs. Today, such screening is illegal.

The following is a guide to legal and illegal questions asked during the employment interview.

1) About the applicant's name **you may ask:**

Have you ever used another name in your work?

You may not ask:

What is your maiden name?

What is your spouse's maiden name?

2) About the applicant's address **you may ask:**

What is your present address?

You may not ask:

Do you own your own home?

3) About the applicant's age **you may ask:**

Are you of legal age? (If the job involves work forbidden to minors, you must ask if the applicant is at least of minimum age.) Do you have a work permit?

You may not ask:

How old are you?

What year were you born?

When did you graduate from high school?

How old are your children?

Do you plan to retire soon?

4) About the applicant's citizenship **you may ask:**

Are you a U.S. citizen?

Are you authorized to work in the United States?

Are you authorized to remain permanently in the United States?

You may not ask:

In what country do you have citizenship?

Are you a native of the United States?

When did you receive U.S. citizenship?

Do you have naturalization papers?

Are your parents, spouse, or children U.S. citizens?

5) About the applicant's national origin **you may ask:**

Are you a U.S. citizen?

Do you speak a foreign language? (This question must be job related.)

You may not ask:

What is your nationality or ancestry?

Highlight

You may not ask:
- How old are you?
- What year were you born?
- When did you graduate from high school?
- How old are your children?

What is your native language?

6) About the applicant's race **you may ask:**

Do you voluntarily wish to identify yourself as a minority to help this employer meet affirmative action goals? (Note: this question must be asked of all applicants, not just obvious minorities)

You may not ask:

To what race do you belong?

What color is your skin?

Could you send a photo of yourself?

Are you of mixed racial heritage?

What race is your spouse or parents?

7) About the applicant's religion **you may not ask** any questions during the pre-hiring process. Once the applicant is hired, **you may ask** if any religious accommodations need to be made.

8) About the applicant's gender **you may ask:**

Do you voluntarily wish to identify yourself as a female to help this employer meet affirmative action guidelines?

You may not ask:

Do you feel this job will be harder for you because you are a woman?

Do you plan to raise a family or become pregnant anytime soon?

What are your childcare arrangements?

9) About the applicant's marital status **you may not ask** any questions until the applicant has been hired

10) About the applicant's sexual orientation **you may not ask** any questions before or after the applicant is hired.

11) About the applicant's disability **you may ask:**

Do you wish to voluntarily identify yourself as a disabled individual to help this employer meet affirmative action goals? (This question must be asked of all applicants, not just of obviously disabled people.)

What accommodation might be necessary to help you perform this job? (You may not disqualify someone because he or she needs to have special accommodations.)

Highlight

You may not ask:

- What are your childcare arrangements?

You may not ask:

Do you have a disability?

Have you been tested for AIDS or have you taken AIDS drugs such as AZT?

Why are you in a wheelchair?

How severe is your disability? (Unless it might be impossible to perform the job safely and efficiently with that disability.)

Will you take a pre-employment physical? (May be asked only if the work is very strenuous.)

Have you ever collected workers comp?

12) About the applicant's military service **you may ask:**

Do you wish to voluntarily identify yourself as a veteran for reporting purposes? Must be asked of all applicants.

You may not ask:

Have you ever served with a branch of the U.S. Armed Forces? (Unless this question directly relates to the present job.)

Did you receive an honorable discharge?

Are you a military reservist?

13) About the applicant's arrest record **you may ask:**

Have you ever been convicted of a felony?

What were the exact charges?

When were you convicted?

Did you undergo rehabilitative counseling?

You may not ask:

Have you ever been arrested? (Being arrested does not mean a person committed a crime.)

14) About the applicant's memberships **you may ask:**

Do you belong to any relevant professional or trade organizations?

You may not ask:

To what religious, political, or social clubs do you belong?

15) Third-party Questions: You may not ask a third party any questions about the applicant that you would not ask the applicant yourself.

Highlight

Sometimes it is not the question that is illegal, but how it is asked.

Sometimes it is not the question that is illegal, but how it is asked. For example, asking about a person's race, gender, disability, or veteran status is illegal. However, if all applicants are asked whether they would voluntarily identify themselves as members of these groups for reporting purposes only, then it is allowed. (This information must be kept in a file separate from the employee's personnel file.)

Highlight

Companies may also protect themselves by clearly stating on the application that it is not an employment contract, and that filling it out does not guarantee an applicant will be hired.

At what point a question is asked is another important factor. Inquiring whether someone is married during the interview or on a job application is illegal. However, once he or she is hired, questions about family may be asked for benefits and tax purposes. What is important to the EEOC is that an employer does not discriminate when hiring or firing.

Questions are not the only way to get into trouble during an interview. Humor that is racist, sexist, or otherwise biased has no place in the employee interview.

Interviewing is a two-way street. An applicant will ask the employer about company policy regarding job reviews, promotions, raises, training opportunities, and termination rights. Many personnel agencies advise applicants to delay asking about salary and benefits until they are actually offered a job, or until the final interview. Employers who deal fairly with their employees should not mind answering these questions. If possible, the applicant should get a written job description, including responsibilities, hours, wages, and benefits. This helps avoid possible misunderstandings later.

Promises and disclaimers

Employers should be careful about written promises, particularly those made on application forms. Promises the company makes on a written job application may be used against the company later in a breach of contract suit. Avoid unnecessary statements regarding company policy and employee benefits.

Some companies include a statement that employment is contingent upon the applicant passing a pre-employment physical. Companies may also protect themselves by clearly stating on the application that it is not an employment contract, and that filling it out does not guarantee an applicant will be hired. Such a legal disclaimer could prove useful if a breach of contract suit should arise.

Background checks

Some employers have stopped relying solely on interviews and applications, and have turned to private investigators to run background checks on senior-level applicants. However, these types of background checks are illegal in many states.

An important rule for employers to remember is that all questions of applicants, whether part of an interview, application, or credit/reference check, should be asked only out of strict business necessity. This is the legal standard most courts use and the one that a company will have to meet if an applicant files a lawsuit against it.

Pre-employment testing

Although the laws regarding the acceptability and applicability of pre-employment tests are constantly evolving, there are six areas where problems most often occur.

1) Polygraph tests

Pre-employment polygraph or lie detector tests are legal in a job involving:

- security
- state, local, or federal law enforcement
- nuclear power
- public transportation
- sensitive information

Under no circumstances may applicants be asked about their racial, religious, sexual, political, or union beliefs while taking a lie detector test. If lie detector tests are used, they must be given to all applicants for the position. Both the employer and the applicant may wish to consult an attorney before a lie detector test takes place, so that both parties may be informed of their legal rights and responsibilities.

2) Drug tests

An employer may give a pre-employment drug test to applicants if all applicants for the same position are tested and if notice is given ahead of time (e.g. on the job application) that drug testing is a condition of employment. The test may not be given, however, until the applicant has actually been offered a job, which itself may be conditional on the test's result. If

Highlight

An employer may give a pre-employment drug test to applicants if all applicants for the same position are tested and if notice is given ahead of time (e.g. on the job application) that drug testing is a condition of employment.

the drug test result is positive, a second test must be given for verification.

3) Pre-employment physicals

No physical exam may be required before an applicant is offered a job (this is a requirement of the Americans with Disabilities Act). However, a job may be offered conditionally, based upon passing a medical exam. Such an exam is legal if:

a. The results are kept private.

b. A business necessity justifies giving such an exam.

c. The exam focuses on the applicant's ability to do the job and not upon any disability.

d. All job applicants for a position are required to take the same exam.

Managers in the applicant's department may not be told the results of the exam unless special work accommodations must be made. Special accommodation means that the employer must provide an otherwise qualified but disabled applicant with the means to do a job, unless an undue business hardship would result.

A physical fitness exam, however, is not considered a medical exam and therefore may be legally required in the pre-employment stages. Such physical fitness exams typically include physical agility, running or lifting tasks. The employer may not measure biological or physical responses to the test.

Employers may refuse to hire a disabled job applicant if the essential job functions would be dangerous to that applicant, or if the applicant presents a safety threat to other employees.

4) HIV testing

Testing for AIDS as a pre-employment condition is illegal unless the position is in healthcare or some other high-risk occupation where close physical contact occurs. No employee outside of a high-risk occupation should submit to employer-requested HIV testing or feel forced to tell an employer of his or her HIV status.

5) English language testing

English language testing may only be used if the job requires superior English language skills. Otherwise, such testing is illegal because it discriminates against immigrants and minorities.

Highlight

No employee outside of a high-risk occupation should submit to employer - requested HIV testing or feel forced to tell an employer of his or her HIV status.

6) Aptitude and psychological tests

As other pre-employment testing becomes illegal, many employers are turning to standardized tests. But these must not reveal evidence of a psychological disorder or impairment. The test may measure personality traits, habits, intelligence and talents. The majority of such tests are controversial. Because the accuracy of such tests can be challenged, an employer relying upon standardized testing must proceed carefully.

Standardized tests must be given under similar testing conditions to all applicants for the same position. Tests may not affect certain groups adversely or favorably. If the hiring rate for a minority group based on tests is less than 80 percent of the hiring rate for the most-hired majority group, the EEOC considers the test to be biased and will force the employer to discontinue use of that test. Employers should send for the EEOC's "Uniform Guidelines on Employment Selection Procedures." This can be obtained by writing to The U.S. Equal Employment Opportunity Commission, Washington, D.C. 20507. Since this demonstrates to the EEOC that a company cares enough to find out the rules, sending for these guidelines could work in the company's favor if an applicant later files an unfair testing lawsuit.

Highlight

Since this demonstrates to the EEOC that a company cares enough to find out the rules, sending for these guidelines could work in the company's favor if an applicant later files an unfair testing lawsuit.

The only purposes of standardized testing should be:

a. To screen out less-qualified applicants

b. To group applicants by ability level

c. To hire those with the best scores

The tests must be statistically valid, and the cutoff scores must be reasonable for applicants at that level. An employer may not test applicants for positions other than those for which they have applied. Some employers claim they are testing applicants for future promotions. Unless the company promotes the majority of its employees within a reasonably short time, e.g. five years after hiring, promotion testing is not legal.

Employers who intend to rely primarily on standardized testing for job selection should have their company attorney review the tests.

Checking references

This guide has already stated that private investigations of an applicant's background could be illegal. However, there is nothing wrong with an employer asking for three or more references from every job applicant. In fact, the employer who wants to protect his or her company will make a point to ask for such references.

Several recent lawsuits have been successfully argued against companies for negligent hiring practices. These practices included hiring employees who were not qualified for a position, or hiring employees with criminal records who went on to commit crimes while in their new firm's employ. If a company requests references, it should check them.

Checking citizenship

Illegal immigration has become a burning issue in the workplace. The 1986 Immigration Reform and Control Act tightened the rules for employers, forcing them to check each new employee's citizenship and right to work in the United States. The law provides stiff penalties for any employer who knowingly hires an illegal alien.

Employers must require all new employees to present proof of both citizenship and their identity. Discrimination in hiring because someone looks or sounds like an immigrant or has a foreign-sounding name is illegal. Even when an employer is certain of a new employee's citizenship, the Employment Eligibility Verification Form I-9 (available from the local Immigration and Naturalization Service office) has to be filled out as proof of citizenship for that worker.

Documents that constitute proof of citizenship status include:
- A birth or naturalization certificate
- A valid U.S. passport
- A valid foreign passport authorizing the person to work in the United States (e.g. a work visa)
- A green card authorizing work in the United States

If none of the above first-choice documents are available, the applicant may present both a Social Security Card and a valid driver's license.

The following documents may be used to prove identity:
- A valid U.S. passport
- A valid driver's license
- A Certificate of U.S. Naturalization or Citizenship
- A school I.D. card with photo
- A draft card or military I.D. card
- A military dependent's I.D. card
- A voter registration card

• A U.S. Coast Guard I.D. card

• Native American tribal forms

The employer should photocopy all identity and citizenship documents and keep the photocopies on file for at least three years. Employees hired before November 6, 1986, who have worked regularly for the company since then are excluded from citizenship checks.

An employer does not have to check the validity of documents presented by employees. If a document appears to be genuine, the employer cannot be held responsible for its possible forgery unless there was reason to suspect that it was not real.

New employees have up to three business days to prove their identity and citizenship. If an alien worker shows a work visa as proof of identity, an employer must be sure that type of visa authorizes work in the job area for which the applicant is being hired. The employer must keep track of the visa expiration, because the alien worker may not be employed beyond that date. (For more information on hiring foreign employees, see the *E-Z Legal Guide to Immigration.*)

Occasionally an employer will discriminate by refusing to hire an alien. If a foreigner feels he or she was wrongly denied employment despite having legal status to work, remedies are available. He or she must file a complaint with the Immigration and Naturalization Service, giving the name of the employer and other pertinent information. The foreigner must be able to prove a pattern of discrimination by that employer to win such a case. If the employer is convicted, he or she faces penalties of at least $10,000. While a private lawsuit may also be filed against the employer, a foreigner should first consult with an attorney.

Employee handbooks and orientation

All new employees should meet with a personnel officer before starting their jobs to discuss wages, benefits, and tax matters. In addition to providing each new employee with a job description, many companies give out a company handbook. Increasingly, employees are filing and often winning breach of contract suits based on promises made in these handbooks.

Most of the handbooks qualifying as contracts contain language guaranteeing employees the following:

1) A particular salary or benefit

Highlight

All new employees should meet with a personnel officer before starting their jobs to discuss wages, benefits, and tax matters.

2) Employment for a minimum length of time

3) Regular job reviews

4) Termination only after certain disciplinary procedures are enforced

5) Phrases such as "It is our company's policy to....", "just cause," or "permanent positions"

An employer should not include any of the above wording in the company's handbook. If there is a section on disciplinary procedures, the company must follow those procedures. If reasons for termination are stated, it may be difficult to fire employees for reasons not stated in the handbook. (However, a company handbook should state the firm's rules. Otherwise an employee may be able to claim ignorance of the rules if fired.) Unnecessary promises regarding training, raises, reviews, promotions, or job guarantees should be avoided. In general, avoid making promises.

A handbook should include a company profile, pay period information, benefit information, equal opportunity/harassment grievance procedures, overtime rules, dress codes, and paid holiday information. The handbook should be updated for accuracy on a regular basis. New employees should be encouraged to address questions to a personnel officer. The best defense against possible lawsuits is to keep lines of communication open between employees and supervisors.

Employment at will

Most jobs fall under the heading of an employment-at-will contract. This means that the employer has the right to terminate employment at any time, and that the employee may leave upon giving proper notification. It is important that the new employee sign a statement acknowledging receipt of the company policy handbook, and acknowledging that he or she has been hired as an employee-at-will. Such a statement provides the employer with essential protection against breach of contract lawsuits. Employers should also check with their state Department of Labor regarding employment-at-will laws that may affect them. Employees may protect themselves by retaining a copy of the handbook.

One further protection is an official disclaimer stating that the handbook is not to be construed as a legal contract, and that the company reserves the right to terminate employment at will. The disclaimer should be put in a prominent spot at the beginning of the handbook and should be written simply and clearly. Many employers post a copy of the disclaimer

---

Highlight

The best defense against possible lawsuits is to keep lines of communication open between employees and supervisors.

---

on company bulletin boards.

Supervisors need to be careful not to make oral promises to employees that may override or contradict what is stated in the handbook. For example, if a company vice president makes an oral promise of continued employment to a worker and that worker is fired according to rules stated in the handbook, a court may rule that because the vice president was an authority figure, the promise invalidated the handbook and the job guarantee must be upheld.

All new employees need to fill out Withholding Tax Form W-4. Employers should maintain employee tax records for at least four years.

Independent contractors

Independent contractors are workers who create products or perform services for a company, but who are not considered employees. Such people do not have income taxes or Social Security withheld from their paychecks. One of the tests used to determine if someone is an independent contractor involves supervision. If the company dictates not only the end result of a contractor's work, but also how the work is to be done each step of the way, that person is not a contractor, but a company employee who must have taxes withheld. A worker also may be considered an employee if the company pays for tools and materials, or if pay is by the hour instead of by the job. The modern test that the courts use asks the question: Would this "independent contractor's" business be able to continue without the financial support of the company with which it does business? If not, that worker is considered an employee.

Companies that falsely claim an employee as an independent contractor for tax purposes face severe legal penalties. Workers with doubts about their status should contact the I.R.S. In addition, companies may not withhold taxes for volunteers and some seasonal employees. Special tax rules apply to trainees, apprentices, and severely disabled employees.

Highlight

If the company dictates not only the end result of a contractor's work, but also how the work is to be done each step of the way, that person is not a contractor, but a company employee who must have taxes withheld.

CHAPTER

Wages

M any regulations have been passed to protect the incomes of American employees. This chapter describes the laws regulating paychecks, paydays, payers and payees. Both employers and employees must be aware of the rights and obligations these laws created.

The Fair Labor Standards Act (FLSA)

The FLSA requires employers to pay employees at least the hourly minimum wage plus overtime for hours worked beyond 40 hours per week. (In some states, overtime is defined as more than 8 hours per day.) The main intent of the FLSA is to protect unskilled laborers and minors who work by the hour, often in low-paying jobs. The Wage and Hour Division of the U.S. Department of Labor closely monitors wage payments to such employees, since the FLSA is frequently violated by employers.

Not all employees fall under the FLSA's protection. Professional, administrative, and executive employees who are paid a fixed salary rather than an hourly wage are generally excluded from FLSA coverage. These are known as exempt employees. Other employees not covered by the law include volunteers, independent contractors, some commissioned employees, outside salespersons, computer programmers/systems analysts, and family members employed in small family businesses.

Minimum wage

The FLSA distinguishes between federal and state minimum wage. When a state's minimum wage is higher, the FLSA requires employers to pay the higher state wage.

Subminimum wage

Apprentices and trainees may receive a subminimum wage if they do not replace regular company employees and if they have not been guaranteed a job once training ends. A subminimum wage may be at least 50 percent and as high as 85 percent of the prevailing minimum wage. All trainees should receive a copy of the training wage rules before they start. Every year an employer must submit listings of available training positions to the State Department of Labor and also display that list in the workplace for other employees to see.

The following groups may be paid a subminimum wage:

1) **Student trainees**: A company may employ up to six full-time student trainees per workday. The employer must file a work application with the Wage and Hour Division of the Department of Labor attesting that the six-student maximum will be observed and that regular employees will not lose their jobs due to the hiring of students. Student trainees may work up to 40 hours per week when school is not in session and up to 20 hours per week when it is. All student trainees must show proof of acceptance to a recognized academic program. The employer should retain a copy of this proof for three years, and must reapply annually for permission to hire student trainees.

2) **Disabled employees**: Severely disabled employees hired through special needs programs (but not regular employees with disabilities) may also be paid a subminimum wage. However, it must be done with the approval of the State Commissioner of Labor.

3) **Employees receiving tips**: Special wage rules apply to employees receiving tips, such as waitresses, taxi drivers, bartenders, and bellpersons. Most states allow employers to credit 50 percent of an employee's tips toward the minimum wage if the employer permits the employee to retain all of his or her tips. Required 15 percent gratuities are not tips; they are classified as employee gross receipts and may not be credited toward minimum wage. Employees must earn at least the hourly minimum wage, whether through tips alone or a combination of tips and employer compensation.

4) **Domestic employees**: Domestic employees are covered by the FLSA if they earn more than $50 in a calendar quarter, or work more than 8 hours per week in one household. Babysitters and companions for the elderly do not come under FLSA protection.

Highlight

Employees must earn at least the hourly minimum wage, whether through tips alone or a combination of tips and employer compensation.

In most states employers may legally credit the cost of housing, meals, and transportation toward minimum wage. Uniforms, tools, and the cost of material may not be credited.

Workweek

Employers must pay at least minimum wage for all regular workweek hours. Overtime hours cannot be included in minimum wage totals.

Normally a workweek consists of a five-day schedule totalling up to 40 hours, after which overtime must be paid. However, in some professions a different workweek standard applies. When firefighters may be called to work at any time and are restricted from going more than a few miles away from the station during non-working hours, they are considered to be on the job and must be paid for that time.

Employees with irregular hours must also get at least minimum wage, despite the fact that their schedules are not nine to five. Such employees often have a written agreement with their employer guaranteeing a minimum total salary per week. They may not work more than 60 hours in a given workweek. Piece rate employees should also receive at least minimum wage for regular work hours.

During the workweek, an employer may not withhold pay for lateness if it would put an employee below minimum wage. Employers have to pay job-related car mileage costs only when it is necessary to bring an employee's pay up to the minimum wage.

Time spent traveling on the job is considered part of the workweek and must be reimbursed. This does not include an employee's regular commuting time. If an employee has to commute to different work sites every day for the same employer, this travel time is to be included as part of the workweek and must be paid for by the employer. An employee who voluntarily reports to work early will not necessarily be paid for it unless it has been agreed to in writing.

Lunch hours and coffee breaks longer than 20 minutes are not part of the paid workweek. However, if the employer requires employees to work while they eat, that time is billable to the employer. Staff training sessions are also considered worktime. The rule for defining an activity as paid work is: if something is being done because the employer wants it done, for his or her benefit, during regular work hours, that activity is part of the workweek and the employer must pay for it.

Overtime

All FLSA-covered employees must receive at least 1 1/2 times their regular hourly pay for each hour of overtime worked beyond a 40-hour week. To determine an employee's regular hourly pay, the employer should add up wages, benefits, vacation pay, sick pay, travel expenses, and profit-sharing plans. This total is then divided by the number of hours in the work-week to get the regular hourly pay rate. The employer must pay 1 1/2 times this rate for any overtime hours worked.

Some employees receive overtime according to a different schedule. Hospital employees receive overtime if they work more than 80 hours during a two-week period. Police officers and firefighters receive overtime if they work more than 212 hours during a 28-day period. Employees who must sleep on the job (e.g. those who work several days on one shift) do not get paid for their sleep time providing that conditions allow a reasonable night's sleep. Employees who are on the job fewer than 24 hours and are allowed to sleep must be paid for their sleep time.

Salespeople working for commission for retail firms do not have to receive overtime pay if their regular hourly pay is at least 1 1/2 times the prevailing minimum wage and if over half of their compensation in a given month is from commissions. A written salary agreement should be in place when the salesperson is hired, defining the hourly rate and how often the salesperson will be paid. This agreement should be signed and dated by both parties.

The Department of Labor limits the total number of hours per week an employee may work. Those in high-risk occupations, such as toxic waste or nuclear power management, have limited overtime.

Highlight

Some employers try to avoid paying overtime by offering their employees compensatory time off instead. It is illegal in most states for a private employer to do this.

Compensatory time

Some employers try to avoid paying overtime by offering their employees compensatory time off instead. Rather than being paid for overtime, an employee takes hours off during the regular workweek. It is illegal in most states for a private employer to do this. Public employers may offer limited (a maximum of 480 hours per year) compensatory time but once an employee works overtime beyond the limit, the employer must pay for the overtime hours worked.

Payday rules

States have different requirements regarding how often payday must occur. In some states it is biweekly or more often; other states allow monthly payments. If an employer states in writing that employees will be paid at certain times, that written agreement is usually enforceable. Employers may change their pay schedule, but must inform employees in advance.

Most states require payment to be in the form of cash, check, or money order payable to the employee, which may be cashed at a local bank. Employees may receive their payments at the workplace or through the mail. Employers may use direct deposit, in which the check goes directly into the employee's bank account on payday. However, such a system must be agreed to in advance by the employee.

Regular wage deductions

Employers may deduct state and local taxes, Social Security, union dues, and unemployment insurance from a paycheck. An employer may also deduct money for premiums on company-paid health insurance, life and disability insurance, and pension plans.

Uniform deductions

The cost of a company-furnished uniform may be deducted from the employee's first paycheck providing the deduction does not put the employee below minimum wage. Employers must reimburse the employee by the following payday. Required dry-cleaning costs for uniforms are the employer's responsibility. However, an employee may not charge an employer laundry costs if the uniform can be washed rather than dry cleaned.

Special wage deductions

There are three special types of wage deductions:

1) **Regular garnishment**: Sometimes an employer is legally required to make deductions from an employee's paycheck for the payment of debts owed by the employee to outside creditors. This type of wage deduction is called a garnishment. An employer has no choice but to comply with such a court order. The employee must be told in advance that garnishment will take place and must have a chance to protest the action.

The Federal Consumer Protection Act allows a maximum of 25 percent of an employee's disposable income to be deducted per paycheck for garnishments. Disposable income is defined as money left from a paycheck once taxes and minimum living expenses are deducted. An employer may not fire or otherwise discipline an employee whose wages are subject to garnishment unless an extraordinary number of overdue debts are owed.

2) **Child support**: Employees may have child support payments deducted from their paychecks. Up to 60 percent of an employee's disposable income may be deducted per paycheck for late child support payments, or up to 50 percent if the employee has a second family to support. If a state law places a stricter limit on what may be deducted, that law must be followed instead of federal law. Child support payments take priority over other garnishments. It is a criminal offense to fire employees because they owe child support. Employers must start withholding child support payments within 14 days of notification by the Child Support Enforcement Agency. They must also tell the agency when an employee owing child support leaves their employ.

3) **Other deductions**: In addition to garnishments and child support, employers may make reasonable paycheck deductions for lodging, meal costs, and loan repayments. However, such deductions may not put the employee below minimum wage.

Recordkeeping requirements

To be in compliance with the FLSA, employers must retain records of employees' earnings for three years. Records should include each employee's name, address, phone, job title, gender, age (in the case of a minor employee), workweeks, pay rate, deductions, and dates wages are paid. There are special recordkeeping requirements for those hiring student trainees, employees receiving tips, domestic employees, and healthcare personnel. The Department of Labor should be contacted for details.

Child labor laws

The FLSA closely regulates work performed by minors. Employers are responsible for verifying the ages of those minors they employ. Employees under 18 (16 in some states) are generally prohibited from performing work involving hazardous waste, such as mining, toxic waste management, and some types of driving. Most states also forbid minors to serve alcohol or work in places that serve alcohol.

Highlight

Employees under 18 (16 in some states) are generally prohibited from performing work involving hazardous waste, such as mining, toxic waste management, and some types of driving.

Minors between ages 14 and 16 may not work during school hours nor after 7 p.m. They may work up to 40 hours per week when there is no school, and up to 18 hours per week when school is in session (before or after school). During summer vacations they may work until 9 p.m. Since state laws are often stricter than federal laws, employees should contact their State Labor Department if there are any questions.

Filing FLSA Claims

Highlight

If, after having met with the personnel officer, the employee still feels the employer is in violation, the employee should consult with an attorney.

Employees who feel their employers have violated one or more provisions of the FLSA may seek legal remedies. The Department of Labor's Wage and Hour Division handles FLSA legal claims. However, due to the number of employers who violate the FLSA, the Wage and Hour Division has many more claims to handle than time allows.

Before an employee complains to the FLSA, he or she should sit down with the company's personnel officer to discuss the issues. If, after having met with the personnel officer, the employee still feels the employer is in violation, the employee should consult with an attorney. The next step is to file a complaint with the DOL, which has officers stationed around the country.

Once a complaint is filed, an officer from the Labor Department will make an inspection of the workplace. If wage violations are found, the employer receives a report that includes a detailed summary of unpaid wages. The employer should always have an attorney or accountant review the accuracy of this report. If the employer does not settle the case by paying back wages, the Department of Labor files charges on the employee's behalf.

Employees can file FLSA claims without fear of employer retaliation. The names of complainants are not usually given to employers. An employer faces severe penalties if an employee is fired for pressing an FLSA suit.

When to file

It is important to file a claim soon after the violation is discovered, because back pay is usually limited to three years. Some employees allow the underpayment of wages to go on for many years, only to discover when they do file a claim that they cannot recover most of what they are owed.

Today, many courts rule in favor of employees who are cheated by their employers. In addition to collecting back pay, an employee who is underpaid may receive damages and attorneys' fees. In addition to collecting back pay, an employee who is underpaid may receive damages and attorney fees.

The Equal Pay Act

The Equal Pay Act, passed in 1963, is an amendment to the FLSA. It requires employers to pay both genders equally for doing similar work. There are only three exceptions to paying equal wages for similar work:

1) If a valid seniority system exists

2) For some types of piece work

3) For merit-based pay systems.

By "similar work" the law does not mean that employees must hold the same job title. Job titles may differ. However, if two employees perform the same type of work for the same number of hours per week, they must be paid equally.

Courts look at four factors when determining similar work:

1) The jobs require equal skill

2) The jobs require equal effort

3) The same amount of responsibility is involved

4) The work conditions are similar

Sometimes job titles are the same but the work involved is different. In this case, the equal pay standard would not apply. For example, if a male administrative assistant handles not only typing but personnel matters and other supervisory duties, and works more hours than the female administrative assistant whose main job is clerical, he may be paid more without violating the Equal Pay Act. (However, if an employer hires only males for higher-level positions that pay more, the employer risks a gender discrimination suit.)

Employers may not lower the pay of the higher-paid employee in cases where wage inequality exists. Instead, the pay of the underpaid employee must be raised. If an employer claims that an employee of one gender is getting paid more because he or she does extra work, the extra work must be necessary and substantial. Benefits and retirement plans must apply to both genders equally. Any firm that claims that one employee is paid more because that employee is the head of a household faces a possible legal challenge in court.

Filing equal pay claims

Two remedies are available to employees who feel they are suffering from pay discrimination because of their gender:

Highlight

Any firm that claims that one employee is paid more because that employee is the head of a household faces a possible legal challenge in court.

1) The employee may contact an attorney and file a private federal lawsuit. Unlike other civil rights violations, the Equal Pay Act does not require claimants to go through the Equal Employment Opportunity Commission before filing claims on their own.

2) The employee may file a claim with the EEOC, realizing that he or she may not then file a private suit unless the EEOC chooses not to pursue the matter. The EEOC will conduct a workplace inspection to check for equal wage violations. If the EEOC finds violations, it will negotiate with the employer to increase pay, reimburse employees of that gender for back pay owed, and force the employer to discontinue unequal pay policies. If the employer refuses, the EEOC may file a lawsuit. If an employee loses his or her job and then wins the lawsuit, he or she may be asked to take a job of equal worth if the old job has been filled. The employee must also be reimbursed for lost seniority and benefits.

Employees may also sue employers under state laws, or, in some cases, under Title VII (see Chapter Four for more information on Title VII cases.) The nature of the proof and the number of employees affected are often factors in deciding the case. The particular state where the lawsuit is filed can also influence the outcome.

Employers convicted of violating the Equal Pay Act may pay penalties of up to $10,000. Repeat offenders are eligible for prison sentences. Although female employees most often face pay discrimination, male employees may file suit if they have proof of wage bias. Employers must base paychecks on ability, education, and experience, and not upon gender stereotypes.

The Agricultural Workers' Protection Act

A federal law exists to protect migrant farm workers from being exploited by their employers. The provisions of this law require anyone hiring migrant farm workers to give them written notice of the following:

- The place of employment
- The type of work
- The present pay rate
- The length of employment
- How wages will be determined (by piecework, etc.)
- Any benefits, including housing and transportation
- Any strikes presently in progress at the worksite

Highlight

Employers must base paychecks on ability, education, and experience, and not upon gender stereotypes.

• Any kickbacks the employer will receive from products

Employers should note that such written statements usually qualify as contracts and must be honored. Employers may not force farm workers to buy goods exclusively from them. They must retain wage records for at least three years after hiring employees, in case of a dispute.

Highlight

Employers may not force farm workers to buy goods exclusively from them.

CHAPTER

Benefits

The benefits a company pays to its employees can be directly translated into money. Most benefits—whether formal or informal, health insurance or a pension plan, child care benefits or a leave of absence – are regulated by state or federal laws. Because questions about benefits are second only to questions about wages among employers, this chapter discusses the rights of both employer and employee concerning benefits, and the laws that govern those rights.

Social Security taxes

All employees, whether salaried or paid hourly, must have Social Security benefits deducted from their paychecks. An employer records each new worker's name and Social Security number when that employee starts employment. The employer and employee each pay 7.65 percent of the employees earnings to Social Security for each month that the employee is employed. Self-employed workers must pay the entire 15.3 percent themselves. These deductions fund several types of programs, including the well-known retirement benefit system.

When an employee reaches the minimum retirement age and has 40 Social Security credits saved up, he or she may retire with full benefits. Employees may also take early retirement and receive a pro-rated portion of their Social Security benefits. Anyone considering retirement should consult with the local Social Security office. It may be worthwhile to remain on the job a few more years to collect the extra money.

Taxes

A Federal Insurance Contributions Act (FICA) tax, used for Social Security purposes, is taken out of each employee's paycheck. Employees who do not have Social Security numbers at the time of employment should apply for them by contacting their nearest Social Security Administration office.

Employers must pay the Federal Unemployment Tax, known as FUTA. Employers must also pay certain state taxes. All employers who provide tax statements to their employees are required to apply for a company tax I.D. number from the I.R.S. The proper application form is available from your local I.R.S. or Social Security office. Employers should also have a copy of the I.R.S. Circular E that details methods for withholding employee income taxes.

Taxes apply to Social Security benefits up to a certain point, after which the benefits become exempt. Since the rules are complicated, both employers and employees should send for the Social Security pamphlet "Part of Your Benefits May Be Taxable."

Highlight

Both employers and employees should send for the Social Security pamphlet "Part of Your Benefits May Be Taxable."

Social Security disability

In addition to retirement benefits, Social Security provides disability payments. The requirements differ from Workers' Compensation requirements because the injury does not have to be work-related. However, the injury must result in total disability. If a person is able to work in any type of job, Social Security will not pay disability benefits. Only permanent injuries qualify for assistance. The employee must have saved up a required minimum amount of Social Security credits by a certain age to qualify. Anyone becoming disabled should contact the local Social Security office for details.

Disabled adult children of Social Security recipients also may qualify for benefits. Adult children must have developed their condition before age 22 and may not start collecting benefits until their covered parent dies, retires, or becomes too disabled to support them.

Non-disabled family members of Social Security recipients may receive Social Security benefits if the recipient is no longer living but was eligible for full retirement (had earned 40 or more Social Security retirement credits). If the recipient was under 28 years old and had earned 6 or more credits before his or her death, the family may still be eligible to collect. There are other situations in which family members are eligible; information is available at the local Social Security office.

Retirees

Retirees collecting Social Security may earn limited wages if they take a job. They are penalized $1 for every $3 they earn above the set earning limit. (There is no earning limit for persons over the age of 70.) Many retirees discover that Social Security does not allow them to live up to their previous standards. Send for the booklet "Estimating Your Social Security Retirement Check," which discusses what an employee can expect to earn when he or she retires.

The Employee Retirement Income Security Act (ERISA)

This federal statute enforces the administration of retirement and benefit plans. Employers do not have to offer employees benefits (except in states where universal healthcare policies require employers with six or more employees to offer health insurance). However, if benefits are offered they must meet ERISA regulations. Employers must file benefit plan descriptions and annual reports with the U.S. Department of Labor and the I.R.S. Copies must also be provided for employees.

The four most common benefit plans governed by ERISA are:

1) Defined benefit plans: These plans require employees to contribute a percentage of their salaries each year toward retirement. If an employee is hired within five years of his or her expected retirement, he or she may be turned down for a defined-benefit plan.

2) Defined contribution plans: These are individual, company-paid retirement accounts in the employee's name. When such plans include profit-sharing, the company contributes a percentage of profits to the employee's account. The employee matches contributions through his or her paycheck. The amount of money in the account when the employee retires determines his or her pension.

3) Stock-option plans: These plans offer employees stock or the right to buy shares in the company. A popular alternative is the 401K plan, which allows an employee to put a percentage of gross earnings into a trust account. No tax is paid on the amount placed in the trust nor on any accrued earnings.

Highlight

Retirees collecting Social Security are penalized $1 for every $3 they earn above the set earning limit.

4) IRAs and Keoghs: Self-employed persons may choose to invest their funds in Keogh plans or Individual Retirement Accounts (IRAs). Some employers also offer their employees IRA accounts.

All company-paid plans are administered through the U.S. Department of Labor, the U.S. Treasury Department, the I.R.S., and the Pension Benefit Guaranty Corporation. If an employer knowingly violates the provisions of a retirement plan, it can result in penalties of up to $100,000 and up to a year in prison.

If a retirement plan is offered to company employees, all employees over age 21 who have worked for the company for at least one year are eligible to participate.

Employers must file their plan descriptions and reports with the U.S. Department of Labor and the I.R.S. Employees must also receive a copy. When an employee leaves, the employer informs the I.R.S. of that employee's pension status. The I.R.S., in turn, gives this information to the Social Security Administration, which handles retirement records.

Vesting

Most pension plans feature some type of vesting procedure, in which an employee slowly accrues the rights to the employer's contribution to the pension account. Some plans use cliff vesting, which means employees don't become vested until they have worked five years for their employer. At that time they become 100 percent vested. With gradual vesting employees are 20 percent vested in a retirement program after three years on the job. They receive an additional 20 percent each year, becoming fully vested when they have been employed for seven years.

An employee not yet fully vested who takes a leave of absence for fewer than five years keeps his or her time already accrued toward full vesting. The limit for retaining accrued time toward full vesting for parental leaves of absence is 501 hours.

An employer may not fire an employee because he or she is about to become fully vested. Employers who do this face damages and lawyers' fees, and have to reinstate the employee.

An employer may modify the pension plan, providing the modification does not interfere with the accumulated benefits of vested employees. If an employer ends the plan, all vested benefits must be paid. However, employees may only receive benefits owed up to the point the plan ended.

Highlight

If a retirement plan is offered to company employees, all employees over age 21 who have worked for the company for at least one year are eligible to participate.

They may not receive the full amount that they would have received upon retiring had the plan remained in place.

Health insurance

Employers providing health insurance must offer it to all employees, regardless of their age or physical condition. If participation in the plan is mandatory, some employees may not be singled out for higher premiums because of age or other factors. If participation is voluntary, higher premiums may be charged, in accordance with established rates.

Any employee who feels he or she has been unfairly singled out for higher premiums should speak with the plan administrator. If still not satisfied, he or she should contact the State Commission on Insurance. Note that it is legal for some employers in some states to limit coverage of pre-existing conditions. However, it is not legal to discriminate against disabled employees. (For more information on disabled employees' rights, see Chapter 4.)

Once an employer promises health benefits in writing, the offer may not be canceled. Before an employer changes insurers or policies, all employees must be notified. Since health benefit rules vary widely, employers should check with their State Health Commissioner for updates.

There are ways for employers to cut down on their healthcare costs. Pre-admission testing, required second opinions, on-site fitness centers, and voluntary wellness workshops are options that may encourage employees to lead healthier lifestyles and avoid unnecessary medical procedures.

Consolidated Omnibus Budget Reconciliation Act (COBRA)

The COBRA law requires companies with 20 or more employees to offer employees and their immediate families an 18-month extension of their healthcare coverage when their employment ends (unless the employee was fired for gross misconduct). Coverage for spouses and dependents may be extended up to 36 months upon the death, divorce, or legal separation of the covered employee.

Highlight

Pre-admission testing, required second opinions, on-site fitness centers, and voluntary wellness workshops are options that may encourage employees to lead healthier lifestyles and avoid unnecessary medical procedures.

Employers must inform employees of their COBRA coverage rights when they enroll in an employer-sponsored health plan, as well as when their employment ends. If the employer fails to inform the employee of his or her COBRA rights, the employer may be held liable for all medical claims that result from the lack of health coverage. Employees have up to 60 days after notification to enroll in the COBRA plan, and 45 days beyond that to make the first payment. Note that the employee pays all insurance premiums. The employer pays nothing, even though the employee continues to be enrolled in the employer's healthcare plan. The advantage to the employee is the opportunity to pay lower premiums because of group rates.

No employee may be turned down for COBRA coverage due to a pre-existing health condition. The only employees not covered, aside from those who work for firms with fewer than 20 employees, are those employed by the federal government, some religious institutions, and the District of Columbia. If a firm has fewer than 20 employees, employees may still be covered under a state COBRA plan.

Individual COBRA policies

If an employee remains uninsured when COBRA coverage expires, he or she must be offered the chance to buy an individual policy with the insurer, regardless of any pre-existing conditions. Such policies are usually very expensive. However, for employees with pre-existing conditions, this may be the best or only choice available. Employers must contact the employees at the time their COBRA coverage expires to notify them of this option.

Military reservists lose their COBRA coverage while on active duty because they are covered by the military during this time. However, upon returning to their jobs, their coverage is reinstated. Disabled employees may receive COBRA coverage for up to 29 months. Both groups have the option to buy individual policies when their coverage runs out.

COBRA death benefits

If an employee dies while receiving COBRA benefits, the immediate family members continue to be eligible for benefits. The plan administrator must inform dependents within 14 days of their rights to continued coverage. The dependents have 60 days to elect to continue coverage and up to 45 days beyond that to pay the first premium.

COBRA-covered employees should immediately notify the plan

Highlight

If an employee remains uninsured when COBRA coverage expires, he or she must be offered the chance to buy an individual policy with the insurer, regardless of any pre-existing conditions.

administrator of any change of address or marital status, or when a dependent child reaches legal age. Estranged spouses of COBRA recipients may also still be eligible for benefits.

COBRA violations

The I.R.S. keeps track of COBRA administration and violations. Employers who fail to inform employees of their rights or otherwise violate COBRA policies may face the loss of federal income tax benefits. They may have to pay up to $100 per person for damages plus attorneys' fees, and may be responsible for any resulting medical claims.

If an employee turns down COBRA coverage, he or she must sign a release and file it with the plan administrator. This release ensures that an employee who later changes his or her mind cannot claim the company failed to provide information about coverage.

Child care benefits

In response to the needs of working parents, many employers are reducing child care-related absences by providing on-site daycare centers. Most on-site child care centers fall under the jurisdiction of ERISA. Once a daycare arrangement has been promised in writing by the employer, it is usually enforceable. Qualified daycare personnel must be hired, and the child care site must meet all state and federal safety regulations. An alternative to providing on-site child care is a Child Care Expense Account. Employees who need daycare for their children may arrange to have a specified amount deducted from each paycheck. This amount then goes to pay for off-site child care. As a bonus, the amount deducted is not subject to income taxes.

The Family Leave Act

Employers with 50 or more employees must offer full-time employees up to 12 weeks of paid leave per year to care for a newborn baby or a child or parent who is seriously ill. A seriously ill employee may also be given paid leave to care for him or herself if it is impossible to work.

Pregnant women and others on parental leave must receive the same accumulated vacation time and pay increases they would receive if they were working. The benefits given to employees with short-term disabilities should be made available to pregnant employees. Those taking parental

Highlight

An alternative to providing on-site child care is a Child Care Expense Account.

leave may not be asked to use up their vacation or sick time before taking their leave. If a firm offers paid leave for non-work-related education or travel, the firm must offer the same amount of leave to new parents for infant care.

Note that the term "parental leave" refers to parents of both genders. Men whose wives are expecting babies or who have a sick child or parent are entitled to the same amount of time off as female employees. Those who adopt children have the same rights.

Employees must have worked for their employer for at least 1,250 hours during the previous 12 months in order to get their job (or one of equal status) back upon their return from a leave of absence. The only exceptions are persons in senior-level management whose leave of absence would seriously hurt the firm's economic well-being. Such employees may risk losing their jobs if they take prolonged leaves of absence.

If the firm is located in a state whose Family Leave law permits more than 12 weeks off, the state law must be honored in place of the federal law. Employees who lose their jobs because they take allowed leaves of absence may sue their employers. An employer may hire someone else for that position only if the employee has clearly indicated that he or she is not returning to work.

Military leave

Those required to take time off to serve in the military as reservists, whether they have been employed by a company for ten days or ten years, must have their jobs held for them until they return. If this is not possible, they must receive a job of equal status upon their return. This protection applies only to full-time employees.

Employees needing military leaves should make their requests in writing. An employer may not require an employee to use up vacation time while performing military duty.

Reservists have up to 90 days after they return from military duty to reapply for their old jobs. If injured while serving, the time limit is extended to one year and 31 days. Military reservists may not be discharged from their jobs for one year after their return. Otherwise, the employer may be charged with retaliation against the employee for having taken time off. Any employer firing a military reservist for just cause must provide extensive written proof of the reason for firing.

Highlight

Note that the term "parental leave" refers to parents of both genders.

Employers must allow reservists to attend all drills and training sessions. Some state laws require employers to pay reservists 14 days worth of wages during their time off. Even if not required to do so, many firms that can afford to pay the wages do so. However, employers who do pay reservists their wages must pay all reservists their wages.

If an employee has been fired or otherwise illegally disciplined for participating in military service, he or she is protected by many laws, including the Veterans Re-employment Rights Act, and should contact the U.S. Department of Labor's Wage and Hour Division.

Highlight

Some state laws require employers to pay reservists 14 days worth of wages during their time off. Even if not required to do so, many firms that can afford to pay the wages do so.

Jury duty

Permanent employees called for federal jury duty are protected from discharge by the Jurors' Protection Act. Many state laws also enforce such protection. If jury duty is for less than a week, exempt employees may not have their salaries reduced. After that, the court usually pays the jurors, and the employer does not have to pay their full salary. Employers who would suffer severe financial hardship by having an employee serve on a jury may apply to the court to have the jury duty postponed.

An employer who fires an employee for serving on a jury faces harsh penalties for violating public policy rules. The employee, however, must have proof that he or she was fired for serving on a jury. Those who are called to court to serve as witnesses are also protected from being fired. Any time an employee receives a court summons, his or her job must be guaranteed by the employer.

Paid holidays and time off

Employers are not required to offer their employees a minimum number of days off per year. Most employers give their employees at least five days off annually for personal reasons, plus federal, state, and religious holidays. Employees should receive this policy in writing when they start their employment. If it is not put in writing, the policy of giving days off is considered informal and may not be enforced in court.

CHAPTER

Privacy in the workplace

Advancements in technology are constantly creating new privacy issues for both employers and employees. Employers need to protect trade secrets and make sure only qualified employees have access to confidential information. Employees must beware of employers who use surveillance and office searches without warning. How much does an employer have the right to know about an employee's private life? Who owns work-related creations? Can an employee be forced to take a polygraph test? Both employers and employees must know their rights in the arena of privacy.

Personnel records

Employers may keep information about employees on file, but only as it relates to business. An employee's personnel file may contain references, job reviews, wage and benefit information, test scores, job-related notices, evaluations, releases, and warnings. It may not contain any mention of race, gender, or disability. Since the Equal Employment Opportunity Commission (EEOC) may request this information, it must be kept separate from an employee's personnel file.

An employee may have access to his or her personnel file by giving advance written notice to the appropriate department. The personnel department has the right to remove any material related to criminal investigations from an employee's file prior to releasing that file to the employee. An employee may be required to inspect his or her file in the presence of a company personnel officer to ensure that personnel documents aren't removed or changed.

Sometimes employees find that information contained in their files is incorrect. Employees have the right to object to malicious or false documents placed in their personnel files, whether a clerical error or a serious charge. Such errors should be removed or clearly labeled as false information. If a supervisor refuses to do this, an employee has the right to insert a note in the file explaining his or her interpretation of what happened and why the supervisor's statement is false. The employee's corrections must be clearly visible to those reading the information and may be stapled to the original document.

Access to personnel files is limited to an immediate supervisor and qualified company officials. Courts weigh a company official's need to know against the employee's right to privacy in deciding whether a violation of employee privacy has occurred. If confidential employee information leaks out and damages an employee's reputation, the employer could be charged with defamation.

The only other situation where personnel records may be made available to those within the company occurs when the employee becomes a threat to himself or others. In such cases, the employee's supervisor and other department heads have a right to inspect relevant information in the employee's file.

Highlight

Employees have the right to object to malicious or false documents placed in their personnel files, whether a clerical error or a serious charge.

Medical records

Strict government rules regulate the confidentiality of employees' medical records. These records must be kept separate from the employee's personnel file, and may only be given out with the employee's consent. Managers have a right to know if an employee's disability might require special accommodations or emergency procedures. Otherwise, they should not be informed about employees' medical conditions. Occasionally government agencies will request and may receive medical records in order to check the employer's compliance with the Americans with Disabilities Act (ADA).

Trade secrets

A trade secret is information about a formula or business practice that others do not know. A secret recipe for cookie dough is an example of a trade secret. Some unique computer programs also qualify, as do patents pending approval.

Many employees believe that if they create a new invention while on the job, they own it. This is not true. If an item was created for an employer during work hours and it qualifies as a trade secret, it legally belongs to the employer. An employee who creates or has knowledge of a trade secret does not have the right to use this knowledge for the benefit of another employer. This is the area where most trade secret disagreements arise.

Nondisclosure agreements

Many employers are now requiring employees to sign agreements stating that they will not divulge company trade secrets if they leave the company. Employers may even ask employees not to take a similar job in the same field or geographic area for a specific number of years. Sometimes an employee will be paid to agree to this. If the agreement is fair and the employee signs it, it is usually enforceable in court. Employees should always check with a qualified attorney before signing such an agreement.

Employees who violate agreements by revealing trade secrets face lawsuits. Even if they did not sign a legally enforceable agreement, it is still illegal to reveal trade secrets. However, employers must be able to prove that the idea was unique and that their legitimate business interests were hurt by the former employee's revelation of the secret.

Ownership

Difficulties may arise when determining when the trade secret was invented. If a employee created a trade secret on his or her own time and with his or her own money, it may be that employee's property, not the employer's. Some employees claim that they had the original idea for a trade secret while on the job but did not invent anything until they were no longer working for that employer. If an employee is able to prove that the trade secret was not developed until after he or she left the job, the court may rule that the trade secret belongs to the employee and that it may be marketed or sold to a new company.

Copyrights

Written and artistic works may be protected by obtaining a copyright from the U.S. Office of Copyrights in Washington, D.C. Technically, such works are protected even before a copyright is obtained. They may be protected from the moment they are written, drawn, or recorded. Authors can initially copyright their work by writing the word Copyright, the year, and their name on the work. They may then obtain an official copyright form from the Office of Copyrights, which establishes proof of ownership if a lawsuit arises.

Employers whose employees create many copyright-protected works should prepare a written agreement stating who owns copyrights on products the employee creates. This will eliminate future misunderstandings about who has rights to the products. For more information on copyrights see the *E-Z Legal Guide to Copyrights and Trademarks.*

Patents

Patents give creators of new products the right to sell those products exclusively for 17 years. The U.S. Patent and Trademark Office issues patents for products it determines are original and useful to the general public. The procedure for approval is complicated and may take several years to complete. For this reason it is often wise to hire a patent attorney.

The Shop Right Doctrine gives employers the right to market a patented product if the invention was created on the job and a written agreement exists giving the employer such rights. In many cases the employee still owns the patent, but the employer has the right to market the invention and share any profits with the employee. States have additional statutes dealing with copyrights, patents, and the ownership of trade secrets. Speak to an attorney if trade secrets are an issue for your firm.

Workplace searches

The workplace search is a controversial issue. Many employees feel it is an invasion of privacy for their employer to search their desks, lockers, belongings, or bodies.

The courts have taken the middle ground, ruling that the legality of searches depends on the employee's legitimate expectation of privacy. If an employee is led to believe that his or her desk or other personal office area is off-limits to the employer, there is a legitimate expectation that searches will not occur. Any unannounced search could thus be considered an invasion of privacy in the workplace.

Employers who feel the need to conduct periodic searches must do the following:

1) Give advance warning. If searches are a company policy, state this in your employee handbook. Explain that you have a right as the employer

Highlight

The workplace search is a controversial issue. Many employees feel it is an invasion of privacy for their employer to search their desks, lockers, belongings, or bodies.

to inspect desks, lockers, and other workplace property upon demand. Often, such a warning is enough to dissuade employee theft.

2) Have reasonable suspicion. It is inadvisable to search employees without apparent reason. Never single out an individual employee to be searched without cause. If items have been disappearing and a particular group of employees have access to these items, this could be a valid reason to conduct a search.

Persons employed in security positions are usually the only employees subjected to body searches. Employers should make sure that searches are kept as non-intrusive as possible in order to minimize employee embarrassment and possible lawsuits.

Highlight

If an employer monitors a phone conversation after having received the employee's consent and it becomes apparent the conversation is personal, the employer must hang up immediately or face possible invasion of privacy charges.

Employee surveillance

Increasingly, employers are using technology to track their employees on the job. This is an area of intense controversy. Following are some forms of employee surveillance, both legal and illegal.

1) **Wiretaps**: Title III of the Federal Omnibus Crime Control and Safe Streets Act of 1968 forbids employers from using wiretapping, phone bugs, or interfering with electronic communications. Telephone conversations may be monitored only with employee consent, and only if the conversations pertain to business. If an employer monitors a phone conversation after having received the employee's consent and it becomes apparent the conversation is personal, the employer must hang up immediately or face possible invasion of privacy charges. Face-to-face conversations may not be monitored under any circumstances.

Employers relying upon hidden cameras must be certain not to station those cameras in areas considered private. Hidden cameras should be confined to the office, and employees must be told that they are being filmed. An employer may only film work-related tasks that he or she needs to monitor out of business necessity.

2) **Private investigators**: More and more employers are hiring private investigators to observe employees outside of the workplace, usually in connection with employees' compensation claims. Although this practice is legal, harassment is not. (For more information on employees' compensation issues, see Chapter 5.) Employees who are followed by a private investigator must receive a copy of the investigator's report and have a chance to confront the investigator before being fired.

Unlike private-sector employees, public-sector employees may not be forced to consent to workplace surveillance. Under no circumstances may any employer spy on or otherwise monitor employees' union activities.

3) **Polygraph tests**: As mentioned in Chapter 1, regulations limit the use of polygraph tests on job applicants. Many states are just as strict about giving polygraph tests to employees. In addition to state laws, the Federal Employee Polygraph Protection Act of 1988 forbids the forced testing of employees. The only exceptions occur when:

a. Workplace theft is present, and the employee to be given the test had direct access to the stolen merchandise.

b. The employee works for a state, federal, or local government agency including, but not limited to, the F.B.I. or the Department or Defense.

c. The employee is in a security or safety-related position (e.g. security guard, public transportation official, or nuclear technician).

d. The employee handles sensitive information.

e. The employee handles drugs.

Employees must receive written notice at least 48 hours ahead of the test explaining why the polygraph test is being given. They must also be given written notice of the date, time, and conditions of testing and be informed that they are not required to take the test as a condition of continued employment. The notice must also explain and include:

a. How the information will be used

b. How the job might be affected by the results

c. The employee's right to sue if the test is improperly given

d. A copy of the test questions

The employee must sign and date the notice and return it to the employer.

Questions may not delve into the employee's racial, sexual, religious, or union beliefs. They cannot be degrading to the employee in any way. No questions may be asked during the test that were not given to the employee ahead of time.

Persons administering polygraph tests must be fully licensed and bonded in the employer's state of residence. If a physician testifies that the employee's physical or mental condition might cause the employee to fail the test, the test cannot be given unless the employee voluntarily agrees to take the polygraph test.

Highlight

Employees must receive written notice at least 48 hours ahead of the test explaining why the polygraph test is being given.

Only the employer has the right to see the results of a polygraph test. A present employer may not ask about any polygraph tests that the employee may have taken for previous employers.

Employees who feel their rights were violated by a polygraph test have up to three years to file legal claims. Employers may be liable for civil penalties of up to $10,000. Reinstatement and back wages are possible if the employee was fired.

Highlight

The Americans with Disabilities Act and several state laws have made it more difficult for employers to fire drug-addicted employees.

Testing

Since the courts have ruled against polygraphs, employers are turning to written honesty tests. These tests claim to measure an employee's tendency to be honest in work-related situations. However, the validity of such tests has yet to be established and many of these tests are considered to be culturally biased against minority employees.

The Drug Free Workplace Act of 1988 requires any company with a federal contract to maintain a drug-free workplace. The employer must have a policy forbidding drugs. Employees are required to inform supervisors within five days after having been convicted of a drug charge. This law neither requires nor forbids drug testing. However, employees in sensitive government and safety-related occupations must be tested for drugs. These include defense employees, transportation officials, nuclear technicians, and employees with access to drugs. Persons in such positions may be fired if they fail a drug test and fail to seek rehabilitation for their problem.

Private employers may test an employee for drugs if such a policy existed at the time of hiring. The policy must state that drug tests will be conducted on all employees within the same job category if a reasonable suspicion exists that an employee is abusing drugs. It must also explain the complaint procedure. The employer must still get each employee's consent before any testing takes place.

The Americans with Disabilities Act and several state laws have made it more difficult for employers to fire drug-addicted employees. Persons who are confirmed to be addicted to drugs or alcohol and are seeking help for their problem may be considered disabled individuals. If they continue to perform up to job standards and are receiving help, they may not be fired for failing a drug test. Such employees are protected employees. (Employees refusing to get professional help are not protected by these laws.)

As with any employment-related testing, the results of drug tests must be kept private. Employers who violate testing conditions are liable for damages. Employees belonging to unions may have additional protections regarding drug testing.

Although employers may regulate drugs and alcohol in the workplace, they may not regulate off-duty behavior unless it has a direct effect on work performance. Otherwise, punishment for off-duty activities is an invasion of privacy.

Highlight

Although employers may regulate drugs and alcohol in the workplace, they may not regulate off-duty behavior unless it has a direct effect on work performance.

CHAPTER

Discrimination in the workplace

The Civil Rights Act of 1964 attempted to eliminate gender and race discrimination in the workplace. Title VII of the Act states that no employer may discriminate in hiring, firing, promoting, or giving raises or other benefits because of an employee's race, gender, color, religion, or national origin. While this federal law is limited to employers with 15 or more employees, most states have similar laws affecting all employers.

Disparate treatment

To qualify as a discrimination case, one of two factors must be present. The first is known as disparate, or different, treatment. This type of discrimination occurs when an employee is a member of a protected class. A class may be protected due to race, gender, or some other factor. For example, pregnant women are a protected class. When a member of a protected class is denied a job or a promotion despite being qualified, and that job or promotion is given to a less qualified employee simply because of race, religion, or gender, then there is a case of disparate treatment. The employer made a work-related decision based upon an illegal bias. In this type of case, one employee is affected, and he or she may file a lawsuit in court.

Disparate impact

The second type of discrimination is called disparate impact. While disparate treatment cases are often based upon intentional employer bias toward one employee, disparate impact cases may be unintentional on the employer's part and tend to affect an entire protected class of employees. Disparate impact cases are often caused by a faulty company policy or test, the result of which discriminates against a minority group.

In disparate impact cases, the employer must prove that the discriminatory policy is essential to the business. Otherwise, the EEOC will force the employer to change or eliminate the offending policy

Employees of a protected class who find themselves subjected to discrimination may file a class action suit. They should contact the EEOC state office for details, and consult with a qualified attorney.

An employee has up to 180 days after the violation occurs to file a complaint with the EEOC. The EEOC has an additional 180 days to investigate the matter and either negotiate with or file suit against the employer. If the EEOC feels that the employee has a case but is unable to resolve it within 180 days, it will issue a Right to Sue letter with instructions on how to file the case in court. The employee has 90 days to do so. The legal procedure is the same for all types of discrimination cases.

Racial discrimination

Affirmative action programs were developed to improve employment opportunities for minorities. If a large discrepancy exists in the number of minorities a company employs, an employer should use an affirmative action program when hiring.

One of the best ways to check for inequities in the employee mix is to look at the racial makeup of comparable companies. If there is a shortage of minority employees in the firm, the company may have to begin recruiting, before the EEOC does it for them.

Affirmative action programs are controversial. An employer must be sure that no one group is underrepresented. However, if an employer hires a minority employee to fill an affirmative action slot and he or she is less qualified than a majority applicant, the employer may be charged with reverse discrimination. It is important that an employer hire only well-qualified minority applicants to fill affirmative action positions. An employer may not fire majority employees to make room for affirmative action employees.

Some employers are confused about how many women or minorities they need to hire to fill the "quotas." In fact, there are no fixed minority quotas. The requirements differ according to type, size, and location of the company. For more information on how to meet EEOC hiring and promotion requirements, contact the state affirmative action agency.

Highlight

Affirmative action programs are controversial. If an employer hires a minority employee to fill an affirmative action slot and he or she is less qualified than a majority applicant, the employer may be charged with reverse discrimination.

Even if a company's policies are not discriminatory, the company is still legally responsible for the racial attitudes of its supervisors. Companies should require supervisors to attend company-sponsored diversity workshops. Evidence of willingness to provide such workshops may provide a strong legal defense for the company if someone later files a lawsuit charging discrimination.

Religious discrimination

Employers must meet all reasonable religious requests, unless the request would cause them undue hardship. Religious schools are the only employers who may discriminate against hiring applicants based on their religion. Federal and state agencies must hire persons of all faiths. If an employee's beliefs require the observance of a religious dress code, the employer must allow the employee to wear the necessary items.

Employers should not schedule important events on major religious holidays, especially if those events could affect an employee's opportunity for job advancement. Nor is this a good time to hold a meeting to determine the company's future course. Holding major events on a religious holiday has an exclusionary effect, which penalizes employees of a minority faith for celebrating their holidays.

Employees whose religious beliefs forbid them to pay union dues may give to charitable organizations instead. For further information on religion in the workplace, send for the EEOC booklet, "Guidelines on Discrimination Because of Religion."

National origin discrimination

Employers may not refuse to hire, fail to promote, or fire employees because they look, sound, behave, or have last names that indicate they are foreign or of a certain ethnic descent. An employer may not ask for proof of U.S. citizenship before an employee has been hired.

Even if an employee is not a foreigner, if he or she faces discrimination because a spouse or friends are foreigners, such discrimination is illegal.

Sexual harassment

The definition of sexual harassment in the 1990s has been broadened considerably. Previously, offensive behavior was measured by male standards. Now the courts routinely invoke the Reasonable Woman Standard. If behavior is offensive to the average woman, it may constitute harassment. Behavior must go beyond simple flirtation to qualify as harassment.

What the courts look for in a harassment case is a pattern of behavior that creates a hostile environment for the employee. If a supervisor orders a worker to sleep with him or her to keep the job, watches employees in the restroom, uses sexually abusive language on a regular basis, pinches or otherwise makes advances toward a worker, displays pornographic material in the workplace (e.g. photos or calendars of nude models), discusses sexual exploits during business meetings, or regularly asks the employee to talk about his or her personal life, the stage is set for a lawsuit: the work environment may be considered too hostile for the employee to accomplish his or her regular duties.

Workers intending to file sexual harassment suits need to start collecting evidence early. They should keep any notes of a sexual nature sent to them by co-workers or supervisors, take photos of offensive posters or pornographic materials displayed in the workplace and, if a supervisor makes oral comment, note who else is present (to serve as a witness). They should keep journals, noting the time, place, and type of harassment as it occurs.

Too often, however, it is the person issuing the complaint who is penalized by the company. A complaining employee may face disciplinary action, such as being transferred to a different work location or department.

Sometimes the company may make the employee's life so miserable that he or she feels forced to quit. If harassment is so pervasive that the employee resigns, the courts may not consider this a true resignation. Instead, they may rule that it was a constructive discharge. The employee had no choice but to quit, so the court considers him or her to have been fired. Therefore, the employee is entitled to collect the same benefits other discharged workers collect, including unemployment compensation and continued health benefits.

No matter what the circumstances, sexual harassment suits take a lot of work to win. Even those who do triumph in court find damages for harassment to be small compared with the damages for, say, racial discrimination. Because of this, many lawyers advise their clients to sue for other things in addition to harassment, such as assault or the infliction of emotional distress. It is important to consult a lawyer who is knowledgeable in the area of sexual harassment.

Highlight

If behavior is offensive to the average woman, it may constitute harassment. Behavior must go beyond simple flirtation to qualify as harassment.

The EEOC files suits on behalf of claimants in harassment cases. The EEOC looks at the following factors when determining whether harassment has taken place:

1) The type of harassment (e.g. comments, advances)

2) How frequently it occurs

3) The level of abuse

4) How many people are involved

The EEOC will interview witnesses and attempt to negotiate a settlement if harassment has taken place. If no settlement is possible, the EEOC will file a suit on behalf of the employee. Even if the EEOC chooses not to pursue the matter, the employee has a right to pursue his or her own private suit.

Although the majority of sexual harassment cases are men harassing women, there has been an increase in the number of cases filed by male employees against female employees and supervisors. Many of these are valid complaints; increasingly, male plaintiffs are winning their lawsuits. Same-sex harassment also occurs. No harassment complaint should be ignored by management. If an employee comes forward with a complaint, it should be investigated immediately.

Other gender-based discrimination

As discussed in Chapter 2, the Equal Pay Act protects women from being paid less than men. Employers should make certain that wages, benefits, promotion policies, and pensions are not based on gender.

Pregnant women have the same rights as other temporarily disabled employees. An employer may not require female employees to take time off because they are pregnant, even if the work involves exposure to chemicals which may be hazardous to the fetus. So-called "fetal protection" laws have largely been overturned in the courts. Employees should be informed of possible hazards and be required to sign a liability statement saying they understand the dangers involved in exposure to such chemicals. This could protect the employer later if an employee files a lawsuit because a child is born with genetic defects.

Sexual orientation discrimination

There have always been homosexual employees in the workplace. Many states have passed legislation making it illegal to discriminate against employees because they are or are perceived to be homosexual. Many companies are now pressured to offer benefits to the live-in companions of unmarried employees. Employers must see to it that all employees' off-duty lifestyles remain private, and that gossip and innuendo play no part in employment decisions.

Age discrimination

True age discrimination applies only to employees age 40 and older. If an employer hires a 25-year-old instead of a 35-year-old, the 35-year-old may not sue for age discrimination, even though age may have been a factor. It is legal to lay off an over-40 employee if he or she is replaced by a another over-40 employee. An employer may not ignore minimum age requirements that are enacted by law. For example, if a job is in a bar where alcohol is served, an employer must refuse to hire anyone under legal age.

Employers must offer identical benefits to older employees, per the Older Employees Protection Act of 1990. In the case of health benefits, employers have to pay the same amount in premiums for all employees. Employers may not fire older employees just before they receive retirement pensions. Just cause must be shown for all terminations.

An employee may not be forced to retire before the age of 70 unless the employee is an executive and is entitled to receive an annual company paid retirement benefit of at least $27,000 per year after the age of 65. An employee cannot be forced to retire if he or she is a senior-level executive for two years prior to reaching age 65. The intent of the law is to protect older employees from forced retirement programs. The few exceptions that exist to the blanket protection of this law occur in safety-related or in physically demanding occupations, such as firefighting and law enforcement.

Early retirement

An employer may offer older employees voluntary early retirement. Employees must be given complete information regarding the benefits they will receive and any disadvantages they might incur as a result of taking early retirement. They must also be told if any layoffs are planned in the near future that could have an effect on their employment. However, employers are not allowed to scare employees into taking early retirement by threatening them with layoffs.

Highlight

True age discrimination applies only to employees age 40 and older. If an employer hires a 25-year-old instead of a 35-year-old, the 35-year-old may not sue for age discrimination.

Every early retiree must be given a written waiver that explains:

1) The rights that the early retiree has agreed to waive

2) That the early retiree has been advised to consult with an attorney before signing the waiver

3) That the early retiree has had at least 21 days to consider the offer

4) That the early retiree has at least seven days after signing to revoke the waiver.

Employees who earn unusually high salaries may be let go regardless of age if the employer can prove that the salary causes the firm economic hardship and that the termination is not age-related.

A person over 40 who feels that he or she has a valid discrimination claim should submit the charges to the local EEOC. The complaint must list his or her name, address, telephone number, the name and address of the employer, and a statement of the facts in the case. The EEOC will not usually give out the employee's name to the employer. Claims must be submitted to the EEOC within 180 days of the incident.

The Americans with Disabilities Act (ADA)

The ADA affects employers of 15 or more employees in all types of businesses. The main purpose of the ADA is to protect employees with disabilities from being discriminated against in hiring, promotions, or other job-related matters. A disability is defined as any physical or mental impairment affecting one or more life activities. Anyone with a chronic disease, such as epilepsy or diabetes, is protected. Mental conditions such as depression and schizophrenia are protected, as are disabilities such as blindness, deafness, mobility impairments, and mental retardation.

Not only are those with real disabilities covered, but those perceived as having disabilities. If a person is no longer disabled but the employer continues to see the employee as being disabled, the ADA protects that employee from being discriminated against by the employer, even though there is no true disability. Persons addicted to drugs and alcohol may in some cases be protected by the ADA. (See Chapter 3 for more information.)

Except for food handlers and healthcare employees who work closely with patients, persons with contagious diseases may not be barred from work unless their disease is easily communicable to co-employees.

Workplaces must be accessible to employees with mobility and other impairments unless undue hardship would result for the employer. This may mean installing a ramp or elevator, widening aisles in the workroom to allow for wheelchair access, or putting telephones and other office equipment at wheelchair level.

Disabled persons who feel they have been discriminated against should contact their local EEOC headquarters and consult with an attorney.

Highlight

This may mean installing a ramp or elevator, widening aisles in the workroom to allow for wheelchair access, or putting telephones and other office equipment at wheelchair level.

CHAPTER

Injuries and workers' compensation

Federal and state governments have passed laws to make employers aware of, and to protect employees from, unsafe working conditions, which cost employers millions of dollars in time, money and lowered productivity. In addition to physical suffering, employees injured on the job lose wages and work. To help remedy this, laws have also been passed to provide financial assistance and job protection to employees who become disabled through a job-related injury.

The Occupational Safety and Health Act (OSHA)

OSHA was enacted to make sure companies provide a safe workplace for their employees. It is a federal law that applies to every private employer, regardless of company size, that is engaged in interstate (between states) commerce. Many states have enacted laws that are even stricter than the federal OSHA law. Since these state laws vary, the local OSHA office or the local Industrial Accidents Commission should be consulted for more information.

Employers must provide a workplace free from known hazardous conditions. If hazards are unavoidable, employers are required to provide employees with proper equipment and training to protect themselves from harm. Specific OSHA requirements include:

Equipment – Tools and machinery must be in working order at all times. New employees must be given adequate training on the safe usage of all tools. Employees must observe safety rules around dangerous equipment and must be provided with protective gear. Employers must not permit food, drink, or any unnecessary items in the work area.

Hygiene and sanitation – All food preparation facilities must be kept clean and meet all sanitation code requirements. Food handlers are required to wash their hands after using the restroom and to wear gloves when handling food. Persons with casually communicable diseases (not including AIDS) should never be allowed to handle food directly, even with gloves on. Food products must be stored in areas cold enough to maintain their freshness. All eating areas must be free from exposure to toxic substances.

Noise – Noise levels must be comfortable for employees throughout the day. Employers are required to provide protective headgear when noise from equipment continuously exceeds 85 decibels for more than eight hours. If noise exceeds that level, employers must offer their employees regular hearing checks.

Lighting and room temperature – Lighting must be adequate for employees to see without straining their eyes or risking injury. Room temperature must be kept at a comfortable level.

Restrooms – Employers should have at least one restroom for each 20 employees of the same gender. Hot and cold water, soap and handtowels must be available in all restrooms.

Showers – Employees in occupations requiring them to shower before leaving work must provide one shower for every ten employees of the same gender. Employees must also have separate storage facilities for their everyday clothes and workclothes.

Smoking – Employees may not smoke in elevators. State laws may give employers the power to ban smoking within the workplace altogether, or to limit it to certain areas.

Fire safety and toxic waste – Every employer should have an evacuation plan in case of fire, and have employees practice regular fire drills. A fire extinguisher should be kept within 50 feet of the main work area, and the number of the nearest fire department should be prominently displayed at all times. Large companies must have fire alarms installed on every floor. Sprinkler and alarm systems should be inspected regularly. The employer is responsible for safely disposing of any hazardous materials.

First aid – If the workplace is not within a reasonable distance of a major medical center, a staff member should be trained in emergency procedures and first aid. If employees routinely handle hazardous materials, many companies arrange for a physician on retainer to be available in an emergency.

Highlight

State laws may give employers the power to ban smoking within the workplace altogether, or to limit it to certain areas.

Hazardous chemical rules

OSHA enforcement is strictest in hazardous occupations such as construction, manufacturing, and chemical processing. The Right to Know Law states that employers must inform employees in advance of any hazardous substances they will be handling. Employers may not require their employees to waive their Right to Know about hazardous chemicals. The employer should have a signed receipt stating that each employee has been properly informed about the hazards.

MSDS sheet

Employees must be properly trained in the management of hazardous chemicals and receive an information sheet called an MSDS (Material Safety Data Sheet). An MSDS sheet lists the properties of each chemical and explains what to do in case of accidental exposure. Each chemical must be clearly labeled and must include the manufacturer's name, address, and telephone number. On-site equipment must be available to flush employees' eyes in case of accidental exposure to hazardous chemicals.

Right of inspection

Employees have a right to inspect records regarding chemical exposures. Employers must comply within 15 days after receiving a written request for inspection of records. OSHA inspectors also have the right to inspect chemical exposure records. These records must be maintained and made available for 30 years following any exposure.

Hazardous Communication Plan

Employers must also keep on file a Hazardous Communication Plan that lists all chemicals used in the workplace. The local fire department should be notified if any chemicals are released into the atmosphere. If the company has chemical trade secrets, those chemicals may be registered with the State Labor Commission, which will assign each chemical a number to be used in all future references.

Safety violations

Employers must display a poster in the workplace notifying employees of their OSHA rights. If employees complain that a work area is unsafe, the employer must investigate. Employees are not required to put themselves at risk by working in an unsafe work environment.

Although OSHA inspectors periodically visit workplaces, employees must not depend solely upon OSHA for safety enforcement. Most OSHA inspections take place after a major accident occurs. Therefore, it is often the employee who must initiate an inspection by filing a complaint with OSHA.

Employees who report their employers for safety violations are protected from being fired or otherwise disciplined. If internal company procedures exist for resolving safety complaints, an employee should follow those procedures before reporting anything to OSHA. If an employee decides to report his or her employer, the complaint must be filed within 30 days of the safety violation. An OSHA case can take as long as four years to settle in court.

Injuries in the workplace

Any injury causing a worker to miss more than one week of work is considered serious and must be reported to OSHA within 48 hours of the attending physician's examination. The report must include the worker's name, the type of injury, and all relevant information about the accident. Employers are also required to file weekly reports with their state's labor commissioner, listing any accidents and describing how much workers' compensation is currently being paid.

OSHA requires companies to display for employees a list of all work-related accidents and illnesses that occurred in the past year. This notice, signed and dated by the employer, must be posted by February 1 and must remain on display until March 1.

Workers' compensation

Workers' compensation reimburses employees for job-related medical and hospital bills as well as any salary loss during a period of prolonged recovery. Because an employee cannot sue an employer for an injury and also collect workers' compensation, workers' compensation laws save the legal system from having to litigate thousands of negligence suits each year.

If an employee is injured on the job, he or she must receive immediate medical attention. If the attending physician decides that the employee is unable to return to work for at least seven days, the employer must be notified within 48 hours. In addition, the injured employee must send a writ-

Highlight

If an employee decides to report his or her employer, the complaint must be filed within 30 days of the safety violation. An OSHA case can take as long as four years to settle in court.

ten report to the state Industrial Accidents Commission. This report must provide the employee's name, address, telephone number, the name of the employer, and the date and nature on the accident.

After receiving the accident report, the state commission will hold a hearing to determine if the injured employee is eligible to receive workers' compensation. The employee must not have been drunk or behaved carelessly at the time the injury occurred. If the employee is judged eligible, this hearing will determine how much compensation the employee will receive, and for how long. The employer, who may be present at the meeting, has the right to contest the severity of the injury, and may appeal any decision the commission makes. The amount of workers' compensation received depends upon how severe the injury is. All injuries fall into one of four categories of disability:

1) **Partial temporary disability.** This is a short-term injury and affects only one body part – a broken leg for example. An employer may require the injured employee to take a temporary job doing light work; this will reduce the amount of workers' compensation that must be paid.

2) **Total temporary disability.** Although recovery is expected within a reasonably short period of time, more than one part of the body is injured. At some point in the recovery the employee will be able to do light work and will be required to accept such a position to reduce the amount of workers' compensation that must be paid.

3) **Partial permanent disability.** The employee has permanently lost the function of one part of the body and can reasonably expect some permanent loss in wages as well. The workers' compensation received will be more generous because future earning capacity as well as present disability is taken into account.

4) **Total permanent disability.** A severely injured employee may never be able to hold a job again. Head injuries are common examples of total permanent disability. In such cases, employees may receive up to 500 times their salary.

Temporary injuries receive standard workers' compensation, which is a percentage of weekly salary, including benefits, multiplied by the number of weeks he or she is expected to miss work. If the employee is receiving a pension at the time of the injury, compensation will be reduced according to a set formula. Although workers' compensation pays all work-related medical costs, an injured employee may be required to use the employer's physician.

Highlight

A severely injured employee may never be able to hold a job again. In such cases, employees may receive up to 500 times their salary.

If you miss at least seven days of work, worker's compensation is retroactive to the day of injury. Some states pay for weekends and holidays. An employer must start paying an injured employee within one week of the hearing with the Industrial Accident Commission, unless ordered to do otherwise. Employees should discuss their case with an attorney before agreeing to a set workers' compensation amount.

Re-injury

Many states set aside funds for employees whose injuries flare up when they go back to work. Employers are hesitant to hire applicants who have been injured, fearing that they might re-injure themselves while on the job. However, employers may not ask job applicants whether they are receiving or have ever received workers' compensation.

Employees who are physically able to return to their jobs must be allowed to do so. If there is no job to return to, the employer must continue paying workers' compensation until another job is found with the company.

Family benefits

Sometimes workers' compensation is awarded to families of employees who were killed on the job. Benefits are limited to the maximum the employee would have received if alive but permanently disabled. Widows and widowers are eligible to receive benefits until they remarry. Children under 18 may receive benefits as well. In some states, unmarried persons who are living together may also collect workers' compensation.

Elective and alternate coverage

Most states require employers with 10 or more employees to carry workers' compensation insurance. New Jersey, Texas, and South Carolina are among the few states that make it elective for employers in nonhazardous professions to carry workers' compensation insurance. In these states, when no workers' compensation is available, an injured employee is allowed to file a lawsuit instead.

Some states allow employees to sue their employers, even though those employers have workers' compensation. Since employees who sue and lose may not collect workers' compensation, an employee should be sure of adequate medical coverage before refusing workers' compensation benefits.

Highlight

Employers are hesitant to hire applicants who have been injured, fearing that they might re-injure themselves while on the job. However, employers may not ask job applicants whether they are receiving or have ever received workers' compensation.

Some worker groups are not covered by workers' compensation, but receive benefits under systems particular to their jobs. Longshoremen, railroad employees, and sailors have their own injury insurance. Before taking a job in any of these areas, the applicant should find out who pays for work-related injuries.

Filing lawsuits

In cases of negligence or intentional injury caused by an employer, the worker has the right to sue his or her employer, whether or not workers' compensation is available. For example, an employer forces an employee to use equipment that is known to be faulty, and an injury results. This is considered a reckless and intentional disregard for employee safety.

Employees may also sue third parties that contribute to their accidents. They may sue a manufacturer for making faulty equipment, fellow employees who show willful misconduct, or landlords who provide unsafe workplaces. The employer will often back the employee in such a third party suit because workers' compensation is reduced by the amount of damages won in a court case against a third party. Thus, the employer pays less if the injured employee wins the lawsuit.

The intentional infliction of emotional distress by an employer or third party at work, which results in an employee's emotional breakdown, also provides grounds for a lawsuit.

Highlight

Employees may also sue third parties that contribute to their accidents. They may sue a manufacturer for making faulty equipment, fellow employees who show willful misconduct, or landlords who provide unsafe workplaces.

Labor unions

Labor unions still play a powerful role in the lives of American workers. In many industries, work conditions and wages are negotiated and controlled by large union organizations. This chapter discusses procedures for forming a union, the federal and state rules governing union activities, and how to file a complaint through your union representative. It also outlines the rights of union members, including their rights during strikes, lockouts, and disciplinary hearings.

Forming a union

The National Labor Relations Board (NLRB) decides whether a group qualifies to become a union. It may limit union membership to employees holding specific types of jobs. For example, the manufacturing employees in a company may qualify as a union, but not the non-manufacturing employees, even though they work for the same employer. Sometimes location figures into the NLRB's decision as well. If an employer has many scattered worksites throughout the country, the NLRB may limit the union coverage to employees on the West Coast, with separate unions for regional locations.

Once the NLRB decides a group meets union guidelines, an NLRB representative will conduct a sample election to see if the majority of employees want a union. If more than 30 percent of eligible employees approve, the group files a petition with the NLRB to be recognized as an official union, with the right to hold elections for union representatives. This group must also receive certification from the employer, indicating that the firm has no objection to the organization of a union and that the employer will negotiate for at least one year with elected union representatives.

An employer may not promise false pay raises in order to persuade employees not to join the union. It is also illegal for an employer to threaten to fire employees if they form a union. Employees forming unions are protected from employer retaliation by the National Labor Relations Act (NLRA).

An employer may not form a company union if the union would be under his or her financial control. Such measures are meant to make employees think they have true representation when, in fact, the employer handles all union decisions and gives them no say.

Sometimes employees must choose between competing unions in their industry. The NLRB helps employees make this choice. Once employees select a union to represent them, no group of employees may negotiate with any other union.

Unions do not represent every type of worker. Independent contractors are excluded from union coverage, even if other employees from that firm are represented. Supervisors are usually excluded from union representation as well.

Union employees' rights

All union members have an equal right to vote in elections, to assemble and speak freely, to have a disciplinary hearing with union representation, to distribute union literature outside the employer's property, and to sue the union if it fails to represent members' interests. Employers may not threaten, harass, penalize, or blacklist employees who belong to a union, nor may they question employees about their union activities or past union memberships.

Unions are subject to the same Title VII rules as everyone else. No union member may be discriminated against within the union because of race, color, gender, religion, or national origin.

Most unions require members to pay annual dues. Members have a right to be refunded dues used to further political causes they don't support.

Illegal shops

Several types of union situations are illegal:

Highlight

Employers may not threaten, harass, penalize, or blacklist employees who belong to a union, nor may they question employees about their union activities or past union memberships.

Closed shops are workplaces where only those who are already union members may be hired. The Labor Management Relations Act forbids this type of shop.

Union shops allow non-union employees to be hired, but they must join the union within 30 days of hiring. These are also illegal.

Agency shops do not require employees to join the union, but all employees must still pay union dues. Many states have ruled agency shops to be illegal as well.

The NLRB advises employee groups about individual state laws. The Labor-Management Reporting and Disclosure Act requires unions to file financial statements and bylaws with government offices. Union members may inspect all documents upon request.

The Excelsior List

Within seven days of a union obtaining permission from the NLRB to hold an election, the employer must give the person regulating the election an alphabetical list of the names and addresses of employees who are represented by the union. This list, officially known as an Excelsior List, determines who may vote in a union election. A valid election may not be held without an Excelsior List, and it may not be held until ten days after the list is submitted.

Illegal activities and election challenges

Employers may not interfere with elections by threatening union supporters or spying on their union activities. Intimidating visits to employees' homes before an election are illegal. Employers may not require employees to attend anti-union speeches the day before a union election.

Employers are not the only ones who try to interfere with union elections. Union candidates may not campaign near the polling place and may not slander other candidates. Bribes, threats, and any other coercive behavior by either side, aimed at voting union employees, are illegal and may invalidate an election.

An NLRB representative and observers representing the employees and employer conduct the actual election. Employees whose eligibility to vote is questioned may be challenged at the polling place, and their votes put into sealed envelopes. Eligibility is decided later.

Highlight

Bribes, threats, and any other coercive behavior by either side, aimed at voting union employees, are illegal and may invalidate an election.

After the election, the NLRB representative will issue a Certificate on Conduct of Election signed by all parties and stating that the election was fair. Objections to election results must be filed within seven days after the results have been officially tallied. All parties must receive a copy of the results, with an additional copy sent to the regional NLRB director. The director will investigate any claims of an unfair election. Either the election will be set aside as having been unfair and a new one ordered, or the results will be ruled valid. If valid, no new election may be held for one year.

Collective Bargaining Agreements

Once a union is formed and representatives are elected, those representatives will meet with the employer to develop a Collective Bargaining Agreement. This agreement establishes the payment of wages, benefits, pensions, bonuses, raises, vacations, lunch breaks, and work schedules for employees represented by the union. The agreement may also cover disciplinary and firing procedures for employees, and help to establish safety rules for employees. Most collective bargaining agreements also specify conditions for hearing worker complaints.

Union complaints

Employees must take complaints against their employers to their union representative. The representative will sit down with a company supervisor to discuss the issue in terms of the collective bargaining agreement. If the supervisor does not admit to violating the agreement, the union representative will then meet with a senior supervisor. Sometimes a formal hearing is held to settle the issue, with employee, employer, and union representative present. The employee may have an attorney present at such a hearing if he or she chooses.

Sometimes a neutral third party, called an arbiter, is called in to settle a dispute. The arbitrator may independently check the facts before reaching a final decision. Both parties are bound by the arbitrator's final decision.

While union members may not negotiate their own employment contracts separate from other union members, employers may not disregard union agreements and pay employees by some other standard without union approval.

Strikes, boycotts and lockouts

When a large group of employees has a dispute with the employer, unions may declare an official strike. Employees have a right to go on strike

Highlight

Sometimes a formal hearing is held to settle the issue, with employee, employer, and union representative present. The employee may have an attorney present at such a hearing if he or she chooses.

if that right is stated in the union agreement. However, the employer also has a right to hire temporary employees to replace striking employees until the strike ends.

Employees may picket their employer's premises and encourage boycotts of their employer (but not against firms doing business with their employer). Nonstriking employees have a right to protect their own safety by refusing to cross a picket line or doing anything else that would put them in danger. These rights must be clearly defined in the union agreement. Employees may lose benefits during strikes, but this must be clearly outlined in the benefits plan.

Employers may legally retaliate against strikers by declaring a lockout and shutting down their facilities, ensuring that all employees lose the right to earn a paycheck during the strike. Often such pressure tactics are enough to get union representatives to the bargaining table, and may force them to negotiate in the employer's favor.

Employees who go on strike over safety issues or unfair labor practices must be rehired when the strike is over. If the strike had to do with wages, the employer may refuse to rehire those employees immediately, but must keep them in mind for future job openings. However, an employee who participates in a wage-related strike may find it very hard to get an old job back or be hired for another job with the same employer.

Employers may legally refuse to rehire employees convicted of crimes during strikes or lockouts. Criminal behavior includes trespassing on the employer's property.

The President of the United States has the authority to order a strike to end if it is considered hazardous to the public welfare. Employees may be ordered back to work for up to 80 days, during which time both sides must try to settle the dispute.

Sometimes groups of employees walk off the job in an unorganized strike known as a concerted action. This occurs when employees have safety complaints or need to protest unfair labor practices. If their complaints are valid, the employees may not be fired from their jobs. Individual employees walking off the job are not protected from being fired unless they have been harassed or there is a safety violation. (See Chapter 5 on Discrimination and Chapter 6 on OSHA rules for more information.)

Highlight

Employees may picket their employer's premises and encourage boycotts of their employer. Nonstriking employees have a right to protect their own safety by refusing to cross a picket line or doing anything else that would put them in danger

CHAPTER

Leaving the job

No employer enjoys having to fire an employee. There is often a sense of failure on both sides. Nevertheless, sometimes the cost of benefits or an economic downturn forces employers to terminate positions. This chapter serves as a guide for employment contracts, firings, plant closings and layoffs.

Employee-at-will

Most employees don't realize that they can be fired at any time. Unless there is a formal written contract between employer and employee that clearly states the beginning and termination dates of employment, the employee is considered an employee-at-will. An employee needs to understand his or her work status when a new job is accepted. If an employer refuses to put promises in writing, an applicant must assume that he or she is being hired as an at-will employee, and that the employer has the right to fire for just cause, at any time.

Firing for just cause includes:

Insubordination

> Constant lateness, absences, or drug/alcohol use
>
> Low productivity, poor job performance, or incompetence
>
> Threatening a supervisor or coworker
>
> Fighting with fellow employees
>
> Lying on the job application
>
> Refusal to follow a required dress code
>
> Discriminating against or harassing coworkers

Violating safety rules

Layoffs caused by an economic downturn

Job obsolescence

Wrongful discharge

When an employee is fired without just cause, it is called wrongful discharge. This means the employer fired the employee without reason and was wrong to do it.

Most wrongful discharges occur when an employer:

- Violates an employment contract.
- Fires an employee for reporting a safety violation or an incident of job-related discrimination.
- Violates a good faith relationship with a long-time employee.

Bad-faith firing affects the older, long-time employee who has spent most of his or her career with one company. This employee typically has a strong performance record and may even be one of the company's top wage earners. He or she is often fired when new management takes over and wants to hire younger employees with less expensive health benefits. Sometimes a bad-faith firing occurs because a salesperson is about to collect a large commission. To challenge a bad-faith firing, it is important to be able to prove:

- That the employee had a strong performance record.
- That the employee worked for the same employer for many years.
- That the employee did not deserve to be fired.

Discrimination

The other major reason for wrongful discharge is discrimination. Many employers secretly loathe affirmative action programs, in which a certain number of protected minorities must be hired. If these employers can't find a way not to hire women and minorities, they will find a way to fire them.

How does an employee prove that discrimination was the real reason for having been fired? He or she must create a paper trail, filing any harassing notes, maintaining a journal noting incidents of discrimination, and listing the names of any witnesses to these incidents. The courts will need

Highlight

Bad-faith firing affects the older, long-time employee who has spent most of his or her career with one company. He or she is often fired when new management takes over and wants to hire younger employees with less expensive health benefits.

extensive proof if an employee sues for wrongful discharge based upon discrimination. The burden of proof will be upon the employee, especially if the company has no previous record of wrongful discharge.

Implied contracts

Even if there is no express contract between employer and employee, there may be an informal, implied contract. An implied contract may exist if oral promises were made to the employee by persons in authority, or if promises were printed in the company handbook and the employee relied upon that information.

Perhaps the employer told the applicant before he or she accepted the job that the position would last for at least five years. Maybe the company handbook stated that all employees in a similar position were permanent employees who could only be fired for reasons stated in the handbook. Sometimes a person is recruited from a competitor with promises of job security. These are examples of implied contracts. When they are broken by employers, the result can be wrongful discharge.

Express contracts

Unlike implied contracts, express contracts are formal written documents stating the length of employment and the possible reasons for dismissal. Although they forbid an employer from firing at will, they also prevent an employee from resigning at will. If there is an express contract and the employer fires an employee without cause, there are strong grounds for a lawsuit. Both employer and employee should maintain copies of the contract, job reviews and any warnings given before the firing.

Most employers will try to make it appear that the employee was fired for willful misconduct, thus avoiding a wrongful discharge claim. Willful misconduct consists of repeated instances of extreme behavior, usually insubordination, threats, violence, theft, health or safety violations, lying or participation in an illegal strike. Unless it has a direct effect upon job performance, off-the-job behavior cannot be cited in willful misconduct charges.

Firing hazards

Perhaps an employer has been trying for months to resolve an employee's problems. Although the strategy has included counseling, retraining, and time off, the employer is now convinced that the employee must be fired.

Highlight

If there is an express contract and the employer fires an employee without cause, there are strong grounds for a lawsuit.

In order not to violate company policy, the next step is to discuss the firm's disciplinary and firing procedures with the personnel officer or company attorney. Some company handbooks state, for example, that an employee must first receive an oral warning, followed by a written warning, followed by suspension, before he or she may be fired. Whatever the company procedure is, it must be followed. Otherwise, the company risks a lawsuit.

The company lawyer or personnel officer should attend the actual firing to act as a reliable witness and advise the fired employee of his or her rights regarding COBRA and unemployment compensation. If violence is possible, a security officer should be present.

The employer should be polite, courteous and honest about the reasons for the discharge. The employee must promptly be paid all wages due by the next payday. Any accrued vacation time also must be included in the severance pay.

Plant closings and layoffs

The Workers Adjustment and Retraining Act of 1988 (WARN) was enacted to protect those permanent full-time employees affected by plant closings and layoffs. All employers with 100 or more full-time employees are covered by this law.

WARN requires employers to give their employees at least 60 days notice when more than 50 employees – or 33 percent of the workforce whichever is larger – will lose their jobs.

Notice must be given to the employees' union representative at the time that the employer finds out about the closing or layoffs. Each affected employee must be individually notified if no union exists. The notices should include the name and address of the affected employment site, the planned course of action, which employees will be affected, the dates for termination of employment, and the company official to be contacted for further information. Notices must also be sent to the State Dislocated Employees Office.

If there is a realistic chance of refinancing and saving the company, employers may give fewer than 60 days notice, since once notice is given, lenders might withdraw financing support. Fewer than 60 days notice is also allowed in the case of a natural disaster or the financial collapse of a major contractor.

Highlight

WARN requires employers to give their employees at least 60 days notice when more than 50 employees – or 33 percent of the workforce, whichever is larger – will lose their jobs.

Employers must give additional notice if there is a postponement of the closing or layoffs. If a business owner sells the business, he or she is responsible for giving notice of impending layoffs until the day of the sale. If the need for layoffs does not become evident until after the sale, the buyer must notify all affected employees.

An employee may file a lawsuit against an employer if the employer violates the provisions of WARN. Such employees are entitled to back wages and benefits up to a set limit. State laws may offer employees additional protections and remedies.

Employer bankruptcies

Two bankruptcy options exist for employers who are unable to pay their creditors.

In a Chapter 7 bankruptcy there is no chance of the business surviving. The employer sells all business-related assets and pays the creditors, including employees who are owed back wages.

A Chapter 11 bankruptcy is a plan for the employer to remain in business. The firm reorganizes its debts and pays less than 100 cents on the dollar to each creditor. A creditor's committee is formed, consisting of one representative for each type of creditor. This committee oversees the repayment of debt according to a plan that has been approved by a federal bankruptcy court.

Some creditors have a higher priority than others when being paid in a Chapter 11 bankruptcy. For example, employees who complete their work after the employer files for bankruptcy and thus take a greater risk in not getting paid will be paid before those who completed their work prior to the filing of the bankruptcy. In either case, the employee, who is a creditor, may have to settle for less than 100 cents on the dollar.

Unemployment compensation

Being fired from a job for any reason besides willful misconduct usually entitles the employee to unemployment compensation. The following groups, however, are not eligible:

1) Agricultural workers

2) Independent contractors

3) Former employees of certain religious institutions

Highlight

Employees who complete their work after the employer files for bankruptcy and thus take a greater risk in not getting paid will be paid before those who completed their work prior to the filing of the bankruptcy.

4) Teachers with a reasonable chance to be employed during the following year

5) Voluntary retirees

There are special situations in which those fired for willful misconduct may still collect unemployment compensation. Sometimes an employer fails to understand the definition of willful misconduct.

The employer must establish that company disciplinary rules are clearly stated in writing, and that those rules are applied equally to all employees.

In some states drug or alcohol abuse is considered a disability, not willful misconduct. If an employee can prove that he or she is getting help for the problem, that person cannot usually be denied unemployment compensation. The burden of proof for establishing willful misconduct falls upon the employer.

Highlight

In some states drug or alcohol abuse is considered a disability, not willful misconduct.

The claim process

The unemployed worker must go to the local unemployment office, bringing a notice of discharge. The notice must include the stated reason for leaving the job. The unemployed worker should also bring a Social Security card and one picture I.D.

Before deciding whether the unemployed worker qualifies for benefits, the unemployment office will verify the claim by contacting the person's last employer, who was the firing employer.

If the firing employer challenges the person's right to receive benefits, the unemployment office will hold a formal hearing. At this point, the unemployed worker should hire an attorney, because appeals must be filed within a certain number of days of the initial application for benefits.

Qualifications for Unemployment Compensation

Most states require an employee to have worked for a minimum number of weeks and to have earned a minimum salary before he or she is eligible to collect unemployment compensation. The weekly unemployment check is based upon the maximum wage rate earned during the preceding year. Employees who voluntarily resign must establish just cause in order to receive unemployment compensation. Some states allow a person to collect unemployment compensation if he or she resigned to care for a seriously ill relative. Otherwise, the person has to prove constructive discharge – work conditions were so intolerable that no reasonable person could remain on the job, and there was no choice but to leave.

If an employer fails to keep certain promises, such as for raises or promotions, the employee may also resign and collect unemployment benefits. Sometimes the job for which a person was hired changes drastically, becoming a completely different job. Any employee in these circumstances should consult with an attorney. In order for the unemployed worker to qualify for unemployment benefits, the former employer must have been paying unemployment taxes and have a record of the person's employment. All businesses that employ one or more full- or part-time employees for at least 20 weeks, or who pay more than $1,500 in employee wages, are required to pay unemployment taxes. Non-profit employers must pay unemployment taxes if they employ one or more employees for at least 13 weeks in a year. Employers of domestic servants must pay unemployment taxes if the employee earns more than $1,000 in a quarter.

Persons receiving unemployment compensation do not automatically have income taxes deducted from their checks. Future employers may not ask about unemployment compensation or discriminate against anyone who has received it.

Benefits may be collected for a maximum of 26 weeks in a year but the federal government may choose to extend this limit. Once benefits have been collected for the maximum number of weeks, the person may not begin collecting again until one year from the date of the last collection.

Maintaining eligibility

The unemployment office must have proof that the job seeker has contacted a minimum number of employers each week for that job seeker to maintain eligibility. An entry-level or low-paying job does not have to be accepted if the unemployed person has previously been a senior level executive. The person may also refuse a job outside his or her professional field, a job where there is an ongoing strike, a job to which no reasonable transportation exists, or a job with unusual hours. It constitutes criminal fraud for a person to claim that he or she is looking for work while collecting benefits when not a single prospective employer has been contacted. If a person takes a part-time job or receives payments from an outside source, the weekly unemployment payments will be reduced.

Highlight

It constitutes criminal fraud for a person to claim that he or she is looking for work while collecting benefits when not a single prospective employer has been contacted.

References

The employer must be careful about what he or she tells a former employee's new employer if contacted as a reference. While the facts should be truthfully stated, it is important not to defame the former employee's character. Under no circumstances should a former employee be blacklisted.

Highlight

The employer must be careful about what he or she tells a former employee's new employer if contacted as a reference.

Glossary
of useful terms

A-D

Affirmative action - government guidelines requiring an employer to hire minority employees in order to remedy past employment discrimination.

Arbitration - a legal proceeding whereby both sides of a dispute agree to submit to the decision of an impartial third party, called an arbitrator.

Boycott - to refrain from dealing with a particular business or industry.

Class-action suit - a lawsuit representing all of the employees in a protected class, which is filed against an employer.

Coercion - using threats to force a person to do something.

Collective bargaining agreement - an agreement between an employer and a union that establishes the rights and obligations each has toward the employees.

Concerted action - an unofficial strike, not sanctioned by a union.

Copyright - the protection of original works by authors and artists from unauthorized use or sale by others.

Defamation - an oral or written statement communicated to a third party that damages a person's reputation in the community.

Disclaimer - a clause in a contract that attempts to limit one party's liability in the event of a lawsuit.

E-W

Employment-at-will - an employment relationship in which an employer has the right to fire an employee without notice.

Estranged spouse - a former spouse or a separated spouse.

Express contract - a formal, written contract defining the rights and responsibilities of both parties.

Felony - one of a serious class of crimes punishable by death or imprisonment for a term exceeding one year.

Gender bias - discrimination based upon a person's sex.

Green card - a document issued by the Immigration and Naturalization Service allowing an alien to permanently live and work in the United States.

Head-of-household standard - an illegal pay standard whereby two equally qualified employees with the same job responsibilities are paid unequally because one of them is the head of a household and the other is not.

Illegal alien - a foreigner who has entered the United States illegally.

Just cause - legal justification for firing an employee.

Naturalization certificate - the official document granting U.S. citizenship to a foreigner.

Off-duty behavior - any non-work-related activity.

Patent - the protection of an original invention from the unauthorized use, sale, or manufacture by others.

Polygraph test - a lie detector test.

Pre-existing condition - any medical or health-related condition that existed, and continues to exist, at the start of an employee's health coverage.

Protected class - any group of people based on race, sex, national origin, or religion that is legally protected from discrimination.

Reasonable Woman Standard - behavior considered reasonable to the average woman.

Third party - a party to a lawsuit other than the employer or the employee.

Serious injury - any injury that causes an employee to miss more than one week of work.

Wrongful discharge - firing an employee without just cause.

How To Save On Attorney Fees

Millions of Americans know they need legal protection, whether it's to get agreements in writing, protect themselves from lawsuits, or document business transactions. But too often these basic but important legal matters are neglected because of something else millions of Americans know: legal services are expensive.

They don't have to be. In response to the demand for affordable legal protection and services, there are now specialized clinics that process simple documents. Paralegals help people prepare legal claims on a freelance basis. People find they can handle their own legal affairs with do-it-yourself legal guides and kits. Indeed, this book is a part of this growing trend.

When are these alternatives to a lawyer appropriate? If you hire an attorney, how can you make sure you're getting good advice for a reasonable fee? Most importantly, do you know how to lower your legal expenses?

When there is no alternative

Make no mistake: serious legal matters require a lawyer. The tips in this book can help you reduce your legal fees, but there is no alternative to good professional legal services in certain circumstances:

- When you are charged with a felony, you are a repeat offender, or jail is possible.
- When a substantial amount of money or property is at stake in a lawsuit.
- When you are a party in an adversarial divorce or custody case.
- When you are an alien facing deportation.

Highlight

When are these alternatives to a lawyer appropriate? If you hire an attorney, how can you make sure you're getting good advice for a reasonable fee? Most importantly, do you know how to lower your legal expenses?

- When you are the plaintiff in a personal injury suit that involves large sums of money.
- When you're involved in very important transactions.

Are you sure you want to take it to court?

Consider the following questions before you pursue legal action:

 What are your financial resources?

Money buys experienced attorneys, and experience wins over first-year lawyers and public defenders. Even with a strong case, you may save money by not going to court. Yes, people win millions in court. But for every big winner there are ten plaintiffs who either lose or win so little that litigation wasn't worth their effort.

 Do you have the time and energy for a trial?

Courts are overbooked, and by the time your case is heard your initial zeal may have grown cold. If you can, make a reasonable settlement out of court. On personal matters, like a divorce or custody case, consider the emotional toll on all parties. Any legal case will affect you in some way. You will need time away from work. A newsworthy case may bring press coverage. Your loved ones, too, may face publicity. There is usually good reason to settle most cases quickly, quietly, and economically.

 How can you settle your disputes without litigation?

Consider *mediation.* In mediation, each party pays half the mediator's fee and, together, they attempt to work out a compromise informally. *Binding arbitration* is another alternative. For a small fee, a trained specialist serves as judge, hears both sides, and hands down a ruling that both parties have agreed to accept.

So you need an attorney

Having done your best to avoid litigation, if you still find yourself headed for court, you will need an attorney. To get the right attorney at a reasonable cost, be guided by these four questions:

 What type of case is it?

You don't seek a foot doctor for a toothache. Find an attorney experienced in your type of legal problem. If you can get recommendations from clients who have recently won similar cases, do so.

Highlight

Even with a strong case, you may save money by not going to court.

Where will the trial be held?

You want a lawyer familiar with that court system and one who knows the court personnel and the local protocol—which can vary from one locality to another.

 Should you hire a large or small firm?

Hiring a senior partner at a large and prestigious law firm sounds reassuring, but chances are the actual work will be handled by associates – at high rates. Small firms may give your case more attention but, with fewer resources, take longer to get the work done.

 What can you afford?

Hire an attorney you can afford, of course, but know what a fee quote includes. High fees may reflect a firm's luxurious offices, high-paid staff and unmonitored expenses, while low estimates may mean "unexpected" costs later. Ask for a written estimate of all costs and anticipated expenses.

How to find a good lawyer

Whether you need an attorney quickly or you're simply open to future possibilities, here are seven nontraditional methods for finding your lawyer:

1. *Word of mouth:* Successful lawyers develop reputations. Your friends, business associates and other professionals are potential referral sources. But beware of hiring a friend. Keep the client-attorney relationship strictly business.

2. *Directories:* The Yellow Pages and the Martin-Hubbell Lawyer Directory (in your local library) can help you locate a lawyer with the right education, background and expertise for your case.

3. *Databases:* A paralegal should be able to run a quick computer search of local attorneys for you using the Westlaw or Lexis database.

4. *State bar association:* Bar associations are listed in phone books. Along with lawyer referrals, your bar association can direct you to low-cost legal clinics or specialists in your area.

5. *Law schools:* Did you know that a legal clinic run by a law school gives law students hands-on experience? This may fit your legal needs. A third-year law student loaded with enthusiasm and a little experience might fill the bill quite inexpensively—or even for free.

6. *Advertisements:* Ads are a lawyer's business card. If a "TV attorney" seems to have a good track record with your kind of case, why not call? Just don't be swayed by the glamour of a high-

Highlight

High fees may reflect a firm's luxurious offices, high-paid staff and unmonitored expenses, while low estimates may mean "unexpected" costs later.

profile attorney.

7. *Your own ad:* A small ad describing the qualifications and legal expertise you're seeking, placed in a local bar association journal, may get you just the lead you need.

How to hire and work with your attorney

No matter how you hear about an attorney, you must interview him or her in person. Call the office during business hours and ask to speak to the attorney directly. Then explain your case briefly and mention how you obtained the attorney's name. If the attorney sounds interested and knowledgeable, arrange for a visit.

The ten-point visit:

1. Note the address. This is a good indication of the rates to expect.

2. Note the condition of the offices. File-laden desks and poorly maintained work space may indicate a poorly run firm.

3. Look for up-to-date computer equipment and an adequate complement of support personnel.

4. Note the appearance of the attorney. How will he or she impress a judge or jury?

5. Is the attorney attentive? Does the attorney take notes, ask questions, follow up on points you've mentioned?

6. Ask what schools he or she has graduated from, and feel free to check credentials with the state bar association.

7. Does the attorney have a good track record with your type of case?

8. Does he or she explain legal terms to you in plain English?

9. Are the firm's costs reasonable?

10. Will the attorney provide references?

Hiring the attorney

Having chosen your attorney, make sure all the terms are agreeable. Send letters to any other attorneys you have interviewed, thanking them for their time and interest in your case and explaining that you have retained another attorney's services.

Highlight

Explain your case briefly and mention how you obtained the attorney's name. If the attorney sounds interested and knowledgeable, arrange for a visit.

Request a letter from your new attorney outlining your retainer agreement. The letter should list all fees you will be responsible for as well as the billing arrangement. Did you arrange to pay in installments? This should be noted in your retainer agreement.

Controlling legal costs

Legal fees and expenses can get out of control easily, but the client who is willing to put in the effort can keep legal costs manageable. Work out a budget with your attorney. Create a timeline for your case. Estimate the costs involved in each step.

Highlight

Don't be afraid to question legal bills. It's your case and your money!

Legal fees can be straightforward. Some lawyers charge a fixed rate for a specific project. Others charge contingency fees (they collect a percentage of your recovery, usually 35-50 percent, if you win and nothing if you lose). But most attorneys prefer to bill by the hour. Expenses can run the gamut, with one hourly charge for taking depositions and another for making copies.

Have your attorney give you a list of charges for services rendered and an itemized monthly bill. The bill should explain the service performed, who performed the work, when the service was provided, how long it took, and how the service benefits your case.

Ample opportunity abounds in legal billing for dishonesty and greed. There is also plenty of opportunity for knowledgeable clients to cut their bills significantly if they know what to look for. Asking the right questions and setting limits on fees is smart and can save you a bundle. Don't be afraid to question legal bills. It's your case and your money!

When the bill arrives

- *Retainer fees:* You should already have a written retainer agreement. Ideally, the retainer fee applies toward case costs, and your agreement puts that in writing. Protect yourself by escrowing the retainer fee until the case has been handled to your satisfaction.
- *Office visit charges:* Track your case and all documents, correspondence, and bills. Diary all dates, deadlines and questions you want to ask your attorney during your next office visit. This keeps expensive office visits focused and productive, with more accomplished in less time. If your attorney charges less for phone consultations than office visits, reserve visits for those tasks that must be done in person.

- *Phone bills:* This is where itemized bills are essential. Who made the call, who was spoken to, what was discussed, when was the call made, and how long did it last? Question any charges that seem unnecessary or excessive (over 60 minutes).

- *Administrative costs:* Your case may involve hundreds, if not thousands, of documents: motions, affidavits, depositions, interrogatories, bills, memoranda, and letters. Are they all necessary? Understand your attorney's case strategy before paying for an endless stream of costly documents.

- *Associate and paralegal fees:* Note in your retainer agreement which staff people will have access to your file. Then you'll have an informed and efficient staff working on your case, and you'll recognize their names on your bill. Of course, your attorney should handle the important part of your case, but less costly paralegals or associates may handle routine matters more economically. Note: Some firms expect their associates to meet a quota of billable hours, although the time spent is not always warranted. Review your bill. Does the time spent make sense for the document in question? Are several staff involved in matters that should be handled by one person? Don't be afraid to ask questions. And withhold payment until you have satisfactory answers.

- *Court stenographer fees:* Depositions and court hearings require costly transcripts and stenographers. This means added expenses. Keep an eye on these costs.

- *Copying charges:* Your retainer fee should limit the number of copies made of your complete file. This is in your legal interest, because multiple files mean multiple chances others may access your confidential information. It is also in your financial interest, because copying costs can be astronomical.

- *Fax costs:* As with the phone and copier, the fax can easily run up costs. Set a limit.

- *Postage charges:* Be aware of how much it costs to send a legal document overnight, or a registered letter. Offer to pick up or deliver expensive items when it makes sense.

- *Filing fees:* Make it clear to your attorney that you want to minimize the number of court filings in your case. Watch your bill and question any filing that seems unnecessary.

- *Document production fee:* Turning over documents to your

Highlight

Note in your retainer agreement which staff people will have access to your file. Then you'll have an informed and efficient staff working on your case, and you'll recognize their names on your bill.

opponent is mandatory and expensive. If you're faced with reproducing boxes of documents, consider having the job done by a commercial firm rather than your attorney's office.

- *Research and investigations:* Pay only for photographs that can be used in court. Can you hire a photographer at a lower rate than what your attorney charges? Reserve that right in your retainer agreement. Database research can also be extensive and expensive; if your attorney uses Westlaw or Nexis, set limits on the research you will pay for.

- *Expert witnesses:* Question your attorney if you are expected to pay for more than a reasonable number of expert witnesses. Limit the number to what is essential to your case.

- *Technology costs:* Avoid videos, tape recordings, and graphics if you can use old-fashioned diagrams to illustrate your case.

- *Travel expenses:* Travel expenses for those connected to your case can be quite costly unless you set a maximum budget. Check all travel-related items on your bill, and make sure they are appropriate. Always question why the travel is necessary before you agree to pay for it.

- *Appeals costs:* Losing a case often means an appeal, but weigh the costs involved before you make that decision. If money is at stake, do a cost-benefit analysis to see if an appeal is financially justified.

- *Monetary damages:* Your attorney should be able to help you estimate the total damages you will have to pay if you lose a civil case. Always consider settling out of court rather than proceeding to trial when the trial costs will be high.

- *Surprise costs:* Surprise costs are so routine they're predictable. The judge may impose unexpected court orders on one or both sides, or the opposition will file an unexpected motion that increases your legal costs. Budget a few thousand dollars over what you estimate your case will cost. It usually is needed.

- *Padded expenses:* Assume your costs and expenses are legitimate. But some firms do inflate expenses—office supplies, database searches, copying, postage, phone bills—to bolster their bottom line. Request copies of bills your law firm receives from support services. If you are not the only client represented on a bill, determine those charges related to your case.

Highlight

Surprise costs are so routine they're predictable. Budget a few thousand dollars over what you estimate your case will cost. It usually is needed.

Keeping it legal without a lawyer ▰▰▰▰

The best way to save legal costs is to avoid legal problems. There are hundreds of ways to decrease your chances of lawsuits and other nasty legal encounters. Most simply involve a little common sense. You can also use your own initiative to find and use the variety of self-help legal aid available to consumers.

11 situations in which you may not need a lawyer ▰▰▰▰▰▰▰

1. ***No-fault divorce:*** Married couples with no children, minimal property, and no demands for alimony can take advantage of divorce mediation services. A lawyer should review your divorce agreement before you sign it, but you will have saved a fortune in attorney fees. A marital or family counselor may save a seemingly doomed marriage, or help both parties move beyond anger to a calm settlement. Either way, counseling can save you money.

2. ***Wills:*** Do-it-yourself wills and living trusts are ideal for people with estates of less than $600,000. Even if an attorney reviews your final documents, a will kit allows you to read the documents, ponder your bequests, fill out sample forms, and discuss your wishes with your family at your leisure, without a lawyer's meter running.

3. ***Incorporating:*** Incorporating a small business can be done by any business owner. Your state government office provides the forms and instructions necessary. A visit to your state offices will probably be necessary to perform a business name check. A fee of $100-$200 is usually charged for processing your Articles of Incorporation. The rest is paperwork: filling out forms correctly; holding regular, official meetings; and maintaining accurate records.

4. ***Routine business transactions:*** Copyrights, for example, can be applied for by asking the US Copyright Office for the appropriate forms and brochures. The same is true of the US Patent and Trademark Office. If your business does a great deal of document preparation and research, hire a certified paralegal rather than paying an attorney's rates. Consider mediation or binding arbitration rather than going to court for a business dispute. Hire a human resources/benefits administrator to head off disputes

Highlight

The best way to save legal costs is to avoid legal problems.

concerning discrimination or other employee charges.

5. *Repairing bad credit:* When money matters get out of hand, attorneys and bankruptcy should not be your first solution. Contact a credit counseling organization that will help you work out manageable payment plans so that everyone wins. It can also help you learn to manage your money better. A good company to start with is the Consumer Credit Counseling Service, 1-800-388-2227.

Highlight

If your business does a great deal of document preparation and research, hire a certified paralegal rather than paying an attorney's rates.

6. *Small Claims Court:* For legal grievances amounting to a few thousand dollars in damages, represent yourself in Small Claims Court. There is a small filing fee, forms to fill out, and several court visits necessary. If you can collect evidence, state your case in a clear and logical presentation, and come across as neat, respectful and sincere, you can succeed in Small Claims Court.

7. *Traffic Court:* Like Small Claims Court, Traffic Court may show more compassion to a defendant appearing without an attorney. If you are ticketed for a minor offense and want to take it to court, you will be asked to plead guilty or not guilty. If you plead guilty, you can ask for leniency in sentencing by presenting mitigating circumstances. Bring any witnesses who can support your story, and remember that presentation (some would call it acting ability) is as important as fact.

8. *Residential zoning petition:* If a homeowner wants to open a home business, build an addition, or make other changes that may affect his or her neighborhood, town approval is required. But you don't need a lawyer to fill out a zoning variance application, turn it in, and present your story at a public hearing. Getting local support before the hearing is the best way to assure a positive vote; contact as many neighbors as possible to reassure them that your plans won't adversely affect them or the neighborhood.

9. *Government benefit applications:* Applying for veterans' or unemployment benefits may be daunting, but the process doesn't require legal help. Apply for either immediately upon becoming eligible. Note: If your former employer contests your application for unemployment benefits and you have to defend yourself at a hearing, you may want to consider hiring an attorney.

10. *Receiving government files:* The Freedom of Information Act gives every American the right to receive copies of government information

about him or her. Write a letter to the appropriate state or federal agency, noting the precise information you want. List each document in a separate paragraph. Mention the Freedom of Information Act, and state that you will pay any expenses. Close with your signature and the address the documents should be sent to. An approved request may take six months to arrive. If it is refused on the grounds that the information is classified or violates another's privacy, send a letter of appeal explaining why the released information would not endanger anyone. Enlist the support of your local state or federal representative, if possible, to smooth the approval process.

11. *Citizenship:* Arriving in the United States to work and become a citizen is a process tangled in bureaucratic red tape, but it requires more perseverance than legal assistance. Immigrants can learn how to obtain a "Green Card," under what circumstances they can work, and what the requirements of citizenship are by contacting the Immigration Services or reading a good self-help book.

Save more; it's E-Z

When it comes to saving attorneys' fees, E-Z Legal Forms is the consumer's best friend. America's largest publisher of self-help legal products offers legally valid forms for virtually every situation. E-Z Legal Kits and E-Z Legal Guides include all necessary forms with a simple-to-follow manual of instructions or a layman's book. E-Z Legal Books are a legal library of forms and documents for everyday business and personal needs. E-Z Legal Software provides those same forms on disk for customized documents at the touch of the keyboard.

You can add to your legal savvy and your ability to protect yourself, your loved ones, your business and your property with a range of self-help legal titles available through E-Z Legal Forms. See the product descriptions and order form at the back of this guide.

Highlight

Arriving in the United States to work and become a citizen is a process tangled in bureaucratic red tape, but it requires more perseverance than legal assistance.

(How To Save On Attorney Fees **was compiled and written by Valerie Hope Goldstein.)**

The E•Z Legal Advisor

The book that saves legal fees every time it's opened.

Here, in *The E•Z Legal Advisor*, are fast answers to 90% of the legal questions anyone is ever likely to ask, such as:

- How can I control my neighbor's pet?
- Can I change my name?
- When is a marriage common law?
- When should I incorporate my business?
- Is a child responsible for his bills?
- Who owns a husband's gifts to his wife?
- How do I become a naturalized citizen?
- Should I get my divorce in Nevada?
- Can I write my own will?
- Who is responsible when my son drives my car?
- How does my uncle get a Green Card?
- What are the rights of a non-smoker?
- Do I have to let the police search my car?
- What is sexual harassment?
- When is euthanasia legal?
- What repairs must my landlord make?
- What's the difference between fair criticism and slander?
- When can I get my deposit back?
- Can I sue the federal government?
- Am I responsible for a drunk guest's auto accident?
- Is a hotel liable if it does not honor a reservation?
- Does my car fit the lemon law?

Whether for personal or business use, this 500-page information-packed book helps the layman safeguard his property, avoid disputes, comply with legal obligations, and enforce his rights. Hundreds of cases illustrate thousands of points of law, each clearly and completely explained.

HOME & BUSINESS EDITION

E•Z LEGAL ADVISOR

Fast answers to 90% of your legal questions!

E•Z LEGAL BOOKS

Stock No.: LA101
$24.95 8.5" x 11"
500 pages Soft cover
ISBN 1-56382-101-X

E•Z LEGAL BOOKS®

E·Z Legal Guides

- *Complete information*
- *Full instructions*
- *Do-it-yourself forms*
- *Only $14.95 each*

Living Will & Powers of Attorney

Dying with dignity is on the minds of every baby boomer and every boomer's parents. They are looking for information, for answers, for the forms they need to fill out now, while they are healthy. They'll find it all in one simple book, the *Guide to Living Will & Powers of Attorney*.

Stock No.: G106
$14.95 8.5" x 11"
128 pages Soft cover
ISBN 1-56382-406-X

Immigration

This simple guide explains the various ways America allows aliens to qualify for "green cards," offers step-by-step directions in the petition and application processes, and prepares immigrants to become naturalized citizens. An excellent reference book complete with federally required forms.

Stock No.: G113
$14.95 8.5" x 11"
176 pages Soft cover
ISBN 1-56382-413-2

Divorce

Spouses facing an amicable divorce shouldn't have to face off with contentious lawyers. This guide explains when a do-it-yourself divorce is appropriate, provides the forms necessary, takes the reader through the legal steps, and provides state-by-state information for filing for divorce.

Stock No.: G102
$14.95 8.5" x 11"
160 pages Soft cover
ISBN 1-56382-402-7

Credit Repair

Anyone can improve bad credit with the help of this guide. From discovering exactly what a credit report contains to challenging false information and turning unfavorable reports into glowing reports, it's all in this guide. Sample letters help the reader contact the right authorities and assert his or her consumer rights.

Stock No.: G103
$14.95 8.5" x 11"
176 pages Soft cover
ISBN 1-56382-403-5

Bankruptcy

How does someone file bankruptcy without adding to their debts? With the *E-Z Legal Guide to Bankruptcy*. Takes the confusion out of bankruptcy by taking the reader through the forms, the law, even the state and federal exemptions.

Stock No.: G100
$14.95 8.5" x 11"
128 pages Soft cover
ISBN 1-56382-400-0

Small Claims Court

The reader prepares for his day in court with this guide, which explains the process for the plaintiff and the defendant, offers options to an actual court case, and more. For anyone who has ever thought about taking someone to court.

Stock No.: G109
$14.95 8.5" x 11"
128 pages Soft cover
ISBN 1-56382-409-4

Employment Law

This is a handy reference for anyone with questions about hiring, wages and benefits, privacy, discrimination, injuries, sexual harassment, unions, and unemployment. Written in simple language from the perspectives of both the employer and the employee.

Stock No.: G112
$14.95 8.5",x 11"
112 pages Soft cover
ISBN 1-56382-412-4

Traffic Court

For most American drivers, traffic tickets are an annoying fact of life. But sometimes the motorist doesn't deserve the ticket. This guide tells how and why to fight a ticket, and how to handle a police stop, read a traffic ticket, and take it to court and win.

Stock No.: G110
$14.95 8.5" x 11"
112 pages Soft cover
ISBN 1-56382-410-8

Trademarks and Copyrights

When someone has a great idea and wants to protect it, this book provides the basics of copyright and trademark law: when to get a lawyer, when simply to fill out the right paperwork. Cuts through the volumes of technical information found elsewhere to provide what the layman must know.

Stock No.: G114
$14.95 8.5" x 11"
192 pages Soft cover
ISBN 1-56382-404-3

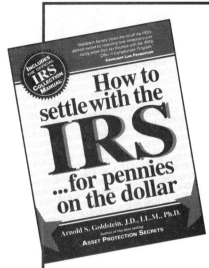

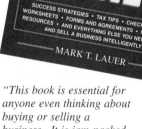

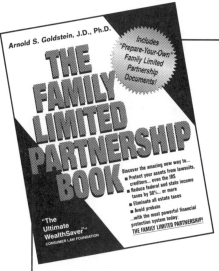

How I Made Millions
with Just a Few Simple Ideas

Stock No.: MILL 500
$19.95 6" x 9"
336 pages Soft cover
ISBN 1-880539-30-6

Turn small ideas into large profits!

Robert M. Hayes

**WHO
HASN'T
HAD
A MILLION-
DOLLAR
IDEA?**

Would-be inventors can take advantage of this well-known author's advice on how to take a simple idea and turn it into MONEY! Covering all phases of modern business, Hayes outlines his hundreds of success stories, and shares inside knowledge that can change failure into triumph.

"The most valuable thing in the world is a good idea...his system shows you how to turn it into MONEY!" **Lloyd MacDonald, Rochester, NY**

"After reading his book, I'm amazed at the wisdom and incredible knowledge covering all phases of modern business." **Beverly Sanders, Ft. Lauderdale, FL**

Super Savvy

Maximize employee performance, productivity and profits with this super book.

Robert E. Levinson

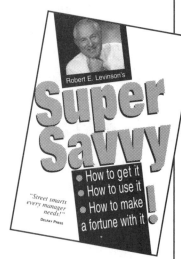

"Street smarts every manager needs"
Delray Press

Levinson's savvy book offers a fresh new approach to "people management" with an insightful perspective on how to get 200 percent from each employee...100 percent of the time. The book teaches modern management principles and emphasizes positive, field tested techniques to get the most out of employees. First-time managers as well as seasoned professionals, can benefit from the principles outlined below:

• Become management savvy and develop team players.
• Be the person everyone comes to for help and advice.
• Spur people to make your goals their goals.
• Spark interest and enthusiasm with job variety.
• Squeeze 70 minutes out of 60.
• Trigger ideas, keep them alive, and translate thoughts into actions.
• Spot the real contributors and develop their potential.
                              ...and more!

Stock No.: SS 400
$14.95 5.5" x 8.5"
256 pages Soft cover
ISBN 1-880539-29-2

 GARRETT PUBLISHING, INC.

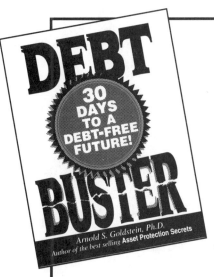

Debt Buster

Stock No.: DBT 600
$24.95   8.5" x 11"
256 pages Soft cover
ISBN 1-880539-26-8

Arnold S. Goldstein, Ph.D.

Debt Buster is a step-by-step guide to getting out of debt without bankruptcy, and managing personal finances efficiently. Here are the solutions for people coping with the daily stress of living from paycheck to paycheck and just making ends meet.

Featured on national television, the Debt Buster program has shown millions of Americans how to:

- Recognize the warning signals of problem debting.
- Protect themselves from bill collectors and negotiate with creditors.
- Use little-known laws to reduce debts.
- Eliminate debt without going broke.
- Avoid bankruptcy, foreclosures, and repossessions.
- Turn credit around, and obtain new credit.
- Protect assets from creditors
  ...and much more!

Guaranteed Credit

Arnold S. Goldstein, Ph.D.

The perfect book for anyone with less-than-perfect credit. In fact, it's for anyone with no credit history, with any type of credit problem, rejected for credit or charge cards, starting over after bankruptcy, who wants to buy a house or car or apply for a bank loan, whose credit is overextended, or who wants more credit for his or her business!

Guaranteed Credit is a practical step-by-step system to establish, repair, or build credit from America's #1 "money doctor" and the man millions of Americans listen to for financial advice. More than a book on improving credit, *Guaranteed Credit* also explains how to get the best deal when you shop for credit. Finally, the author explains how not to abuse..and lose credit.

*Features
a publisher's
money-back guarantee
if credit not improved
after 90 days.*

Stock No.: GC 103
$24.95 8.5" x 11"
256 pages Soft cover
ISBN 1-880539-40-3

 GARRETT PUBLISHING, INC.

Index

S-W

About the Author

Valerie Hope Goldstein earned her B.A. degree at Brandeis University in Waltham, Mass., and her graduate degree in public administration from Brandeis' Florence Heller School of Social Welfare. She received paralegal certification from Northeastern University, with specializations in corporate and probate law.

Ms. Goldstein has acted as a legal and financial consultant for numerous organizations. Presently she serves as content analyst for GTE Main Street, one of the first interactive cable systems in the country.